C000062792

BREAKING INTO THE MOVIES

by
JOHN EMERSON
and
ANITA LOOS
Authors of "How To Write Photoplays"

ILLUSTRATED

PHILADELPHIA
GEORGE W. JACOBS & COMPANY
PUBLISHERS

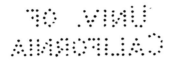

Copyright, 1921, by
THE JAMES A. McCANN COMPANY

All Rights Reserved

PRINTED IN THE U. S. A.

In the interest of creating a more extensive selection of rare historical book reprints, we have chosen to reproduce this title even though it may possibly have occasional imperfections such as missing and blurred pages, missing text, poor pictures, markings, dark backgrounds and other reproduction issues beyond our control. Because this work is culturally important, we have made it available as a part of our commitment to protecting, preserving and promoting the world's literature. Thank you for your understanding.

CASTING THE PICTURE

This is a typical scene in a casting director's office. Mr. Emerson and Miss Loos, with their stenographer, are studying the faces of the applicants. When a type exactly suited to the story is found, she is sent direct to the studio to begin work.

CONTENTS

636296

ILLUSTRATIONS

BREAKING INTO
THE MOVIES

UNIV. OF
CALIFORNIA

Breaking Into the Movies

CHAPTER I

INTRODUCTION

WERE the average man suddenly called upon to assemble all the women in his town who looked like Mary Pickford, he might find himself at a loss as to how to commence. In fact, he might even doubt that there were sufficient persons answering this description to warrant such a campaign.

We know a way to get them all together on twenty-four hours' notice. Just insert a small advertisement in the local newspaper, reading:

"Wanted for the movies—a girl who looks like Mary Pickford—apply at such-and-such a studio to-morrow morning."

We guarantee that not only will every woman who looks like Mary Pickford be on the spot at sunrise, but that a large preponderance of the entire female population will drop in during the morning. For it is a puzzling but indisputable fact that everybody wants to break into the movies.

The curious part of it all is that the movies really need these people.

On the one hand are countless men and women besieging the studio doors in the hope of starting a

1

career in any one of a thousand capacities, from actress to scenario writer, from director to cameraman. There are people with plots, people with inventions, people with new ideas of every conceivable variety, all clamoring for admission. And, on the other hand, there are the men who manage the movies sending out all manner of exhortations, appeals and supplications to just such people to come and work in their studios. They drown each other's voices, the one calling for new talent and new types, the many for a chance to demonstrate that they are just the talent and types that are so in demand.

This economic paradox, this passing in the night of Demand and Supply, has come about through a general misconception of everything concerned with the movies.

The first to be in the wrong were the producers. They built up an industry which, in its early days, was vitally dependent upon individual personalities. A picture, according to their views, was made or unmade by a single star or director or writer, and very naturally they were loath to entrust the fate of a hundred thousand dollar investment to untried hands. While on the one hand they realized the pressing need for new blood in their industry, they were, nevertheless, very wary of being the first to welcome the newcomer. Producers preferred to pay twenty times the price to experienced professionals, no matter how mediocre their work might have been in the past, than to take a chance on a promising beginner. The business side of the movies, has, in the past, been nothing more nor less than a tremendous gamble wherein the men who had staked their fortunes on a single photoplay walked about in fear of their very shadows—desiring new ideas, yet afraid to risk testing them, calling for new artists yet fearing to give them the opportunity to break in. The very nature of the industry was responsible for this situation and, to a large extent, it is a condition which still prevails in a majority of the smaller studios. The greatest obstacle which every beginner must surmount is the one which first confronts him—the privilege of doing his first picture—the first chance.

The larger companies, however, in the last year or so have awakened to the fact that by excluding beginners they have themselves raised the cost of motion picture production many times. They have found themselves with a very limited number of stars and directors and writers and technical men to choose from, all of whom, for this very reason, could demand enormous salaries. One by one these companies are instituting various systems for the encouragement of embryo talent. Now, if ever, is the time to break into the movies.

But much more to blame for the general mix-up in the movies are the beginners themselves. In the majority of cases they state in loud, penetrating accents that they desire to break into the movies, here and now; but when questioned as to the exact capacity in which they desire to accomplish this ambition, they appear to be a bit hazy. Anything with a large salary and short hours will do, they say. The organization of the business and the sordid details connected with the various highly specialized jobs in the studios concern them not at all. They let it go with an unqualified statement that they want to break in the worst way— and generally they do.

Now making movies is not child's play. It is a profession—or rather a combination of professions—which takes time and thought and study. True, there are fortunes to be made for those who will seriously enter this field and study their work as they would study for any other profession. But unfortunately, most of those who head towards the cinema studios do not take time to learn the facts about the industry. They do not look over the multitude of different highly specialized positions which the movies offer and ask themselves for which one they are best suited. They just plunge in, so intent upon making money at the moment that they give no thought at all to the future.

Therefore, in writing this series, we shall start with an old saw—a warning to amateurs to look before they leap. No industry in the world presents so many angles, varying from technical work in the studio, to the complexities of high finance. If you really wish to break into the movies, go to the studios and see for yourself what you are fitted for. Perhaps you think you are an actor, and are really a first rate scenarioist. Perhaps you have an ambition to plan scenery, and instead find that your forte lies in the business office. Men who started as cameramen are now directors. Men who started as directors have ended as highly successful advertising managers. So there you are. You pay your money—and—if you are wise —you take your choice.

CHAPTER II

MOST people seem to think there are concerned in the making of motion pictures just four classes of people—actors, scenario writers, directors and cameramen. It all seems very simple. The scenario writer sits down in the morning and works out a scene; he wakes up the director, who packs some actors and a cameraman in an automobile, together with a picnic lunch, and goes out to make the picture on some lovely hillside. Then, having finished the photoplay, they take it around to your local theater and exhibit it at twenty-five cents a seat.

As a matter of fact, the movies, now the fifth national industry in the United States, has as many phases, and as many complexities as any other industry in the world.

Broadly speaking, the movies are made up of alliances between producing companies and distributing companies. For example, the Constance Talmadge Corporation produces the photoplays in which Miss Talmadge is starred, and this Company is allied with the First National Exhibitors Circuit which takes the completed film and sells it to theater managers in every part of the world. The Constance Talmadge Corporation's duty is to make a photoplay and deliver it to the First National Exhibitors Circuit; the latter company

5

duplicates the film in hundreds of "prints," advertises it, rents it to exhibitors, and sees to the delivery of the film. In the same way, Nazimova makes comedies and releases them through the Metro Corporation, her distributor.

The great distributing companies employ the salesmen, advertising experts, business men, and so forth. All the technical work concerned with the making of the picture, however, is in the hands of the producing company, and, since we are engaged in such work ourselves, it is about these posts that we must talk.

If we are to take the studio jobs in their natural order, the first to begin work on a picture is, of course, the author. Each studio employs a scenario editor who is on the lookout for good magazine stories or plays or original scripts. He himself is not so much a writer as an analyst, who knows what kind of stories his public wants; generally he is an old newspaperman or an ex-magazine editor. Having bought the story, he turns it over to a scenarioist—the "continuity writer." This type of specialist is much in demand, since no story can survive a badly constructed scenario.

The scenario writer puts the story into picture form exactly as a dramatist may put a novel into play form for the stage. It is the scenarioist or continuity writer who really gives to the story its screen value—hence the very large prices paid for this work when it is well done. Next in line is the director, who takes the scenario and sets out to make the picture.

There is a shortage of directors at present, and for that reason, salaries are particularly high in this line, but of course, direction is a profession which takes many years of study.

In beginning work on his picture, the director first consults the studio manager, who is really the head of the employment office. The studio manager consults with him as to the expenses of the scenery and the length of time to be spent in making the picture and then summons the technical staff.

The technical staff of a studio is a rather large assembly. There is the art director, who plans the scenery, the technical man who directs the building, the casting director, who selects the actors, the electrician, who assists in working out the lighting effects, the laboratory superintendent, who must supervise the developing of the film, the cutters, who assemble the completed film, and last, but not least, the cameraman. Of course there are hundreds of minor posts—assistant director, assistant cameraman, property man, research experts, location seekers, and so forth.

The casting director immediately sends out a call for the "types" demanded in the scenario. If possible, he notifies the actors and actresses personally, but more often he is forced to get in touch with them through the numerous agencies which act as brokers in "types." The Actors' Equity Association is now doing excellent work in supplying actors for pictures at the lowest possible cost to the actor in the way of commissions. Presently a large number of actors and actresses appear at the studio and the casting director selects from them the individuals best suited to the coming production. Beginners are warned against grafting agents who on any pretense whatever charge more than the legal 5% commission. They are also warned against signing "exclusion" contracts with any agent, as this frequently compels the actor to pay double commissions.

Meanwhile the art director has built his scenery, and the picture goes "into production." At the end of some six weeks or two months, the directors turn the completed film over to the assembling and cutting department. As a rule both the director and the scenario writer work with the assembler and cutter, and if they are wise, they insist on doing the cutting themselves, for the success of the picture depends largely upon this important operation of assembly. At the same time, another specialist designs and works out the illustrations on the borders of the written inserts. Finally the assembled picture is shown to the studio staff, and if they are satisfied, the negative is forwarded to the distributing company. The studio's work on that picture is ended.

From this brief survey, you can see that the avenues for breaking into the movies are almost unlimited. You can be an actor, director, cameraman, scene builder, cutter, titler, scenario writer, or anything else if you will begin at the bottom and learn the game. All of these positions are highly paid and all require a high knowledge of motion picture technique.

The important thing is to *start*—to get into the studio, in any capacity. Then choose the type of work in which you desire to rise, and learn it. Everybody will help you and encourage you if you start this way, instead of trying the more common but less successful method of starting at the top and working down.

CHAPTER III

ACTING FOR THE SCREEN

IN New York resides a dramatic critic, now on the staff of a great newspaper, who has his own ideas about movie acting. The idea in question is that there is no such thing as movie acting—and the gentleman carries it out by refusing to allow the word "acting" to be printed in any of the notices and reviews in his newspaper. When he wishes to convey the thought that such and such a star acted in such and such a picture he says, "Miss So-and-So posed before the camera in the motion picture."

Now this critic is a good critic, as critics go, but he would be improved physically and mentally by a set of those monkey glands which the medicos are so successfully grafting upon various ossified personalities. Anyone who thinks that there is no such thing as motion picture acting is probably still wondering whether the Germans will win the war. Motion picture acting is a highly developed art, with a technique quite as involved as that of the legitimate stage.

The fundamental principle to remember in undertaking screen acting is that the camera demands far greater realism on the part of the actor than the eyes of an audience. An actor in the spoken drama nearly always overplays or underplays his part. If he recited the same lines in the same tone with the same gestures in real life, he would appear to be just a little bit spiffy, as they say in English drinking circles. On the stage it is necessary to overdraw the character in order to convey a realistic impression to the audience; exact naturalism on the stage would appear as unreal as an unrouged face under a spotlight.

The camera, however, demands absolute realism. Actors must act as naturally and as leisurely as they would in their own homes. Their expressions must be no more pronounced than they would be in real life. Above all, they must be absolutely unconscious of the existence of the camera.

Any deviation from this course leads to the most mortifying results on the screen. The face, enlarged many times life size, becomes clearly that of an actor, rather than a real character. The assumed expression of hate or fear which would seem so natural on the stage is merely grotesque in the film. Unless the actor is really *thinking* the things he is trying to portray on the screen, the audience becomes instantly aware that something is wrong.

In the same way the camera picks up and accentuates every motion on the part of the actor. An unnecessary gesture is not noticed on the stage. On the screen, enlarged many times, it is instantly noted.

The two most important rules to follow, then, in motion picture acting are: act as you would under the same circumstances in real life, and eliminate all movement and gesture which does not bear on the scene. It is better not to move at all than to make a false move.

Beginners must adjust their walk to the camera. There is no rule for this, however, as every individ-

REHEARSING THE COMPANY

Movie authors should rehearse their own stories, at least, according to John Emerson and Anita Loos. Here these authors, on the left, are rehearsing their scenarios for "Wife Insurance" while the director, Victor Fleming (with the cap) takes notes. Rehearsals are arranged before the scenery is built, and the above tableau is supposed to take place in a restaurant.

UNIV. OF
CALIFORNIA

ual's way of standing and walking is different. Only through repeated tests can· the beginner discover and correct the defects which are sure to appear in his physical pose the first time he acts before a camera.

Often in making a picture, the director will instruct his cast to "speed up" or "slow down" their scene. Sometimes, also, he will alter the tempo of the scene by slowing down or speeding up the rate at which the camera is being cranked. Beginners must follow such instructions to the letter, for the timing of a scene is a vitally important part of picture production and a duty which is entirely in the hands of the director.

The best way to learn the principles of motion picture acting is to watch the making of as many scenes as possible before attempting to act one. Most of the stars of to-day learned their art by watching the efforts of others before the camera. Only by constant observation in the studio and, more important, in real life, where the actions and reactions of real people can be noted, can an actor hope to become proficient.

CHAPTER IV

PROBABLY the number of people who have not at one time or another wondered in a sneaking sort of way if they wouldn't look pretty well on the screen is limited to the aborigines of Africa. And, believe it or not, two of the aborigines themselves applied at our studio for jobs not long ago. They had acted in several travelogue pictures, taken in darkest Africa, had traveled as porters with the company to the coast, and had finally become so enamored of the work that they "beat" their way all the way to America, with an English vocabulary limited to about fifty words, twenty-five of which were highly profane. It just goes to show that we are all human. Needless to say, both beauty and character are the characteristics in demand in the films, as everywhere else. The curious fact is that faces which in real life possess great beauty or deep character, frequently fail to carry this across to the camera.

The chief reason for this lies in the fact that the camera does not accept color values, and at the same time accentuates many defects which are ordinarily imperceptible to the eye. For example, a wonderful type of Italian beauty appeared at our studio while we were casting "Mama's Affair" for Constance Talmadge. She had never before appeared in motion pictures, and our casting director was quick to seize the opportunity to make a test of her face. When the picture was shown, her extraordinarily fine coloring of course went for nothing, and her beauty was entirely marred by the inexplicable appearance of a fine down over her upper lip and a large mole on her left temple. Both the mole and the down had been entirely unnoticed in daylight, but under the fierce mercury lights of the studio and the enlarging lenses they made her face grotesque. At another time we attempted to make a leading man of a famous war hero. This boy had been a college athlete and had subsequently distinguished himself as a bayonet fighter on four battlefields. When his test films were projected, to the astonishment of everyone he appeared as an anæmic, effeminate stripling, whose every gesture aroused the ridicule of the audience.

The skin of the face must be entirely smooth and unbroken. The slightest eruption or blemish is visible on the screen, especially in this day when "close-ups" are the vogue. The teeth must be perfect.

Considerations which do not matter in the slightest degree in facial beauty on the screen are those of coloring and of fineness of the features. The pinker a woman's cheeks may be, the hollower they appear to the camera, for red photographs as black, and a face which is beautiful, but coarse in its outline, frequently photographs quite as well as the beautiful face which is exquisite in every detail.

A screen star should be equally beautiful in every expression and from every angle. This is not so true of the stage star, for when she is moving about, speaking and gesticulating, the question of her beauty becomes comparatively unimportant. On the screen, however, important scenes are always taken in "close-ups" wherein the star, whether portraying rage or pain, love or hate, must be equally charming, at the risk of making a permanently bad impression upon her audience.

Many people who are beautiful when seen in "full face" are most unattractive in profile. In fact, the matter narrows down still further, for quite often those who have a lovely profile are, for some inexplicable reason, gross and unattractive when the face is turned to show three-quarters. A number of the present movie stars have risen to the top despite such impediments by stipulating in all their contracts that they be never shown in close-up in the pose in which they are unattractive. One star in particular never shows the left side of her face for this reason. This, however, is obviously a great handicap.

The male types which are most in demand are not those whose appeal is through physical beauty. Audiences are sick of large-eyed, romantic heroes, and are demanding a little manly force and character in their heroes.

To film well, a man's head should be large, rugged, with the features cut in masses, like a Rodin bust. Whether he is attempting to play "juveniles," "leads" or "heavies" his face must possess the cardinal requisites of character. Deep-set eyes, a strong chin, a jutting forehead, a prominent nose, are all desirable. Again, the high cheekbones and long face appear desirable characteristics. William S. Hart's success depends largely on these two simple characteristics of facial structure.

Neither in men nor in women is the hair an essential for screen beauty. Wigs and trick arrangements of the hair are a function of the make-up department, and a man or woman with no hair at all could still be made to appear most attractive to the unsophisticated camera.

In analyzing your own face, then, ask yourself the following questions:

Are my eyes large?

Is my skin fine and well kept?

Is my mouth small and are my teeth good?

Is my nose straight?

Has my face character, something which makes it not only beautiful, but which portrays the underlying personality?

If you can answer these questions in the affirmative you may have a career before you in the motion pictures. If you cannot answer any of them but the last in the affirmative, you may still be successful as a movie actor, for "types"—whether of gunmen or millionaires, villains or saints—are much in demand. One man has made himself a small fortune by playing parts in which a particularly villainous expression were required—such as dope fiends. Another chap, in the Western studios, has made a good living for years by acting "stained glass saints," having been equipped by nature with an unusually æsthetic expression.

In any case, if you are to essay a career in the movies, remember that your natural characteristics are all that count. Tricks of rolling the eyes or puckering the lips or setting the jaw are buncombe and are instantly discovered by the camera.

Be natural. Keep healthy and happy. That, in the movies, as in real life, is the way to charm and beauty.

CHAPTER V

MAKE-UP

ALTHOUGH most women use cosmetics in their every-day life, they are lamentably ignorant of the principles of make-up. For example, not one woman in a hundred knows that she should never rouge her face until she has put on her hat, since the shadow and line of the hat changes the whole color and composition of her face. The average man's knowledge of the subject is limited to the use of powder after shaving. And yet thousands of men and women secure work in the mob and ensemble scenes in the movies and find themselves expected to make up for the camera, the most difficult task of all, with no previous instruction whatsoever. No wonder they are discouraged when they see themselves peering out from the crowd scene with a face they hardly recognize themselves.

Nevertheless, almost all the stars of to-day—Norma Talmadge, Constance Talmadge, Mary Pickford, and dozens of others—have risen from these mob scenes. Their faces, even when seen among hundreds of others, attracted instant attention. Perhaps it was natural beauty. Perhaps, too, they had, by accident or design, solved at the start the great problem which confronts all movie actors, that of finding the correct make-up.

Movie make-up strives only for a photographic

effect and has no relation to street or stage make-up. Almost every face contains numerous imperfections which are invisible to the eye, yet which, when enlarged many times on the screen, are very obvious. There are fundamental rules of make-up, but the only way to perfect your technique is by constantly viewing your own "stills" and movies, and changing your make-up to the best advantage.

Red photographs black, and for this reason rouge is little used in the studios, except for special effects. Rouge on the cheeks gives the illusion of dark shadows and makes the face look hollow; it deepens the eyes, and is sometimes used on the eyelids for this reason. Light carmen may be used on the lips.

To start your make-up you will need cold cream, special yellow film powder, film grease paint, and a soft towel. Massage your face with cold cream and then remove it with the towel, so that the surface is absolutely clean. Then apply your grease paint with the fingers, and cover every bit of the face from the collar-line to the hair.

When you have a smooth, even surface of grease paint, spread special film powder upon it and pat it in lightly with a powder puff. There are a number of shades of grease paint and by changing the grease tint before applying the powder you can darken or lighten your complexion in accordance with your part. Before going further, make sure there are no blotches on your make-up's surface and that the grease has left no sheen.

The eyes are the most important and expressive features. The make-up which relates to them is all important. First you must ascertain by actual test the

ROUGING THE LIPS FOR THE CAMERA

Red photographs black, so particular care must be taken in rouging the lips for movie work. John Emerson is helping May Collins with her make-up, while Anita Loos and the director, Victor Fleming, give suggestions.

CALIFORNIA
UNIV. OF

correct color with which to line your eyes. Almost every color is used, for the effect seems to vary with different faces. Black, blue, green, brown and red are all used in varying proportions and mixtures by different actors. Naturally, you should try to find the color which makes your eyes look deepest and most luminous.

The edge of the upper eyelid is clearly lined. Then the shade is worked back toward the eyebrow, getting constantly lighter, until it finally blends with the grease paint of the face. The process is reversed for the lower lid, which is darkest at the edge and grows lighter as you work down.

Your eyelids should be lined with black cosmetic. Do not bead them. This shows clearly in close-ups and looks rather ridiculous. The slapstick comedy people sometimes use beaded eyelids to burlesque the "baby-doll" expression.

The corners of the eyes are shadowed with brown or red. It is this shadowing that gives most of the character to the eyes; but at the same time it is apt to age the whole face. For this reason it must be done in conjunction with actual tests.

Finally, apply light carmen to your lips and make sure you do not overdo it.

There are numerous special recipes for producing pallor, scars, bruises, and the like. Blackface make-up is done most successfully with charred cork dust mixed with water to produce a heavy paste. Tom Wilson, the best known player of negro parts in the movies, who played in "The Birth of a Nation," and more recently in our own special production, "Red Hot Romance," advises amateurs to use this recipe and, further, to high-light the natural lines of their faces by scraping off the cork with a sharp stick, wherever a line is to show, and letting the natural white of the skin appear.

High-lighting for most character parts is a special art. Such characters as Indian faces or the weather-beaten and wrinkled countenance of an old sea captain may be done in brown with white high-lights. You should ask your cameraman to help you with high-lighting, as it is very difficult.

There are tricks of make-up which alter the entire character of the face. For example, by shading the outline of the face with red you can make it appear much thinner. In this case the grease paint is slightly reddened—or, if you desire, darkened—near the ear-line. If you desire to make your face rounder and fuller reverse the process and lighten the grease paint at its outer edge.

If your eyebrows and hair are dark, you can tinge them gray by rubbing the hair with mascaro and then combing. If they are light, white and black grease paint, applied alternately and then combed, will do the trick. Beards and bushy eyebrows are made of crêpe hair and glued on with spirit gum. As a matter of fact, if you are really serious about making a career of movie acting, it is best to grow, so far as possible, the hirsute appendages required in your parts. For an unshaven tramp or a Robinson Crusoe effect, for example, it is much better to go unshaven for a week or so than to produce a false effect by attempting to imitate the real thing with crêpe hair.

Finally, lest you be left in the position of the man who starts his first ride on a motorcycle without knowing how to shut the power off, we may add that all this nasty mess of grease paint and powder and gum and hair will come off in an instant when cold cream is applied. It is hard to feel natural in make-up at first; but presently you will forget that you have it on at all.

All of the necessary cosmetics may be secured through any drug store or theatrical costumer. If you want to find out how you will look in the movies, it is not necessary to have a film test made. Just buy some make-up and have someone take a few "close-ups" of your head with an ordinary camera. But do not retouch the negatives—for movies are not retouched, you know.

Look for imperfections of every sort in pose and expression. Then try to find a make-up which will eradicate them. If you solve your make-up problem before you go to the studio you will be well repaid. Among the dozens of flat, uninteresting countenances a well made-up face stands out and attracts the attention of the director at once.

CHAPTER VI

HOW TO DRESS FOR A PICTURE

THERE is only one drawback to the pleasurable life of the movie actor or actress. They draw big salaries; they get their names in the papers and are deluged with "fan" letters to such an extent that special postal departments are installed in their offices; the work is interesting and the hours comparatively short. But, alas, they have to have a lot of clothes.

To be sure, the buying of clothes is a most pleasurable experience to all women and to many men. And, forsooth, if they draw big salaries, why cavil about the cost of replenishing a wardrobe every now and again?

The fact is, the wardrobes are not replenished every now and again; they are constantly in a state of replenishment, and for that reason the average actor's bank account, no matter how big the salary, is also in constant need of being similarly replenished. For every new scene is apt to require completely new gowns and suits, and, in the case of the actors who play the more important parts, no two suits or gowns can be worn in any two pictures or the fans will be sure to discover it and write uncomplimentary letters to the studio.

In the case of the beginner, however, no such expenses need be met if he or she has one complete

22

MAKING UP THE EYES

The eyes are the most expressive of the features and their make-up is correspondingly important. Here John Emerson and Anita Loos are helping Basil Sydney, the noted English actor, to darken his eyes in accordance with movie technique.

UNIV. OF
CALIFORNIA

wardrobe to start with. People playing minor characters must dress for the part at their own expense, but no one notices or cares whether they wear the same clothes with which they recently graced the studio next door. If they play a part requiring a special dress or uniform the management will supply it without charge.

It is rather difficult for a newcomer to the movies to know exactly what clothes are required for their wardrobe. Therefore we are including the following comments on clothes and styles, as applied to motion picture work:

Men should have at least three business suits, one of which should be light and one dark.

For summer scenes, white flannels, with a blue coat and a soft shirt—*not* a sport shirt—are required. White duck shoes complete this outfit. Tweed suits are the proper thing for wear in the country club scenes and in most pictures calling for scenes on English estates.

For dress wear three outfits are necessary. There is the cutaway for afternoon weddings, society teas, and so forth, a Tuxedo for club scenes and semi-dress occasions, and finally, full dress for balls and dinners where ladies are in the scene. A dark four-in-hand or bow tie, with a stand-up or wing collar, should be worn with the cutaway, and regulation dress bow ties, black with the dinner coat and white with the dress suit. These clothes are an essential part of a motion picture actor's outfit.

The great difficulty with young actors is a tendency to overdress and to attempt to hide bad tailoring with a flashy design and a freak cut of the coat. Since clothes are an actor's stock in trade, he should patronize only the best, if the most.expensive tailors, and stick to conservative lines unless the part requires eccentric dressing. Jewelry should be avoided, unless called for in the character; cuff links and a watch chain are all that should be worn, with the exception of dress studs with the dinner or dress coat.

Girls will need a simple afternoon suit and an outer coat to match. They must have two summer frocks, a sailor blouse with a dark skirt, negligée, and an evening gown and wraps. Hats to match are necessary, of course, as are dancing slippers and white duck shoes.

The evening gown is perhaps the most important part of the young actress's wardrobe, since she is more apt to be called in for ball and dinner scenes than any other. Simplicity should be the keynote of such gowns. Simple French models are very attractive, but few women can wear them well, since most American girls are too broad in the shoulders for the Parisian styles.

Clothes for character parts must be assembled on the moment according to the demands of the director and the imagination of the actor or actress. Realism is the great essential of character dressing. To wear the rags of a vaudeville tramp in the movies would turn the picture into a slapstick comedy. A real tramp's clothes are a mighty different matter.

The greatest difficulty which a casting director experiences is that of finding people to play the part of society folk. These parts require an understanding of drawing-room manners and ballroom etiquette, and the ability to wear smart clothes. If the clothes are

not up to the moment they will be obsolete when the
picture reaches the country at large, and the audiences
will think that because the styles are out of date the
picture is out of date also.   Also if any extreme
styles are worn they are sure to be out of date when
the picture is shown.   In the same way, the slightest
error in etiquette is sure to be noted and commented
upon.   It is more of a trick than one might think
to know, at a moment's notice, how to act as best man
at a fashionable wedding, or how to serve a ten-course
dinner according to the latest vogue.

The best way is to dress conservatively and to act
as any well bred person might be expected to.   A
man who fails to take off his hat upon entering a
fashionable house would be laughed at.   A man who
took it off with a grand flourish would be hooted out.
Recently a director read in a certain short story that
the Newport set had instituted the custom of supplying a single green glove for each dinner guest to wear
while the olives were served.   This was merely a bit
of satire on the part of the story writer—but the
director took it seriously, and instituted the fad in a
dinner scene with dire results when the picture was
shown to the newspaper critics.

CHAPTER VII

MOVIE MANNERS

THIS chapter does not deal so much with how to act in a picture as how to act in a studio.

Motion picture people live, more or less, in a world of their own. It is a world which may seem a bit topsy turvy to the outsider, with its own peculiar customs, and a greater freedom from restraint than is customary in the conventional world outside. Examined a bit closer, these outlandish ideas appear to be the very same ones which are always associated with artists—a bohemian spirit which is the same whether in Hollywood or the Latin Quarter of Paris.

If the newcomer to the studio wishes to establish himself as a bona fide member of the movie world he must always remember that no matter how cynical they may seem, no matter how pessimistically they may talk, these people, in the bottom of their hearts, consider a photoplay a form of art and themselves as artists. The actor or director or author who does really good work, who has something new to offer, or who at least is sincere in his desire to do something big and fine in the motion pictures, will always be tolerated no matter how bizarre his character in other respects. In short, people are ranked according to their artistic understanding rather than according to their ancestry, their bank account or their morals.

Most of the leaders of the motion picture world have risen from poverty and obscurity, a fact which accounts for the democracy which prevails in the studio.

There are a few rules which beginners would do well to follow. Here they are:

Be modest. Because you don't understand why something is done, don't believe it is all nonsense. And remember that you have ever so much to learn about the business.

Don't criticize.

Try your best to please everyone, particularly the director, whose shoulders are carrying the responsibility for the whole production and whose manner may be a bit gruff—as it usually is when a man is laboring under a heavy load.

Don't be ashamed of being in the movies. If you think movies are a low-brow form of making a living your associates will surely become aware of your state of mind and you will be quietly frozen out.

In the old days of the movies social status in the studio was determined by a curious system, based upon the pay envelope. Actors—for the movie world is composed for the greater part of actors—are classed as stars, the "leads," the "parts," the "bits," the "extras" and "mobs." The star is, of course, the highly paid actor or actress who is the feature of the production; the "lead" is the leading man or woman who plays opposite the star; the "parts" include all those characters which appear on the program—the minor characters of the play; the "bits" are those who are called on to perform a bit of individual action, such as the butler who opens the door, or the chauffeur who drives the car, but who have no real part in the play; the extras are simply members of the crowd, as the ballroom throng, while a mob is just a mass of people, like an army or the audience at a football game.

The large producing companies frequently give elaborate dinners, seating three or four hundred people, and under this ridiculous old system the star sat at the head of the table, with the "leads" near at hand. Then came the "parts," then the "bits," and finally, away down at the foot of the table, were the "extras." In the same way directors, assistant directors, studio managers, and so forth, were graded down according to how much money they drew from the cashier every week.

To-day all this snobbery has passed away. The movie world has its smart set and its slums, as in any other world, but the criterion is artistic worth, not money. We know of one rather unpleasant personality who has risen to stardom, but is completely ignored by the lesser lights of the profession despite this star's attempts to break into "film society."

CHAPTER VIII

On the legitimate stage actors and actresses are called on to read their parts before beginning rehearsals. In the movies the part is read to them. Before the company begins to make even the first scene in a photoplay the scenario writer and director call a meeting and rehearse the company, reading the scenario and explaining the meaning of each scene. If the author and director are wise the story is then carefully rehearsed clear through, scene by scene, before anything is photographed. In this way the actors learn the sequence of their scenes and the relation of their parts to other parts and to the whole.

It is up to you to make the best of your part. Secure a copy of the scenario, or at least of your scenes, as soon as possible. Then go over the story as many times as possible, trying to grasp the relationship of your own character to that of the other characters in the story. Work out your own conception of the part.

Perhaps at first the director will never give you a chance to do a piece of original acting. He will work out every bit of action for you. Eventually, however, your opportunity will come to "create a part," and you must be ready for it.

All the action of a motion picture story is contained in the numbered scenes of the scenario. Your bit of

acting will be in one or more of these scenes. Here
is a sample bit of one of our own scenarios, based
on the stage play "Mama's Affair," which we recently
wrote for Constance Talmadge. These are the last
few scenes of the photoplay:

Eve watches her mother go out, then turns to
the doctor, goes to him, gives him her hand, and
says very quietly:

SP: "GOOD-BY, DOCTOR."
The doctor looks at her, astonished, and says,
"What!" Eve looks up at him sternly and says:

SP: "GOOD-BY; I CAN HARDLY HOPE TO SEE YOU
AGAIN."
She then starts out the door. The doctor hurries
after her, stops her, and says, "What do you
mean?" Eve turns to look at him, and then says
very calmly:

SP: "I SHALL BE LEAVING TO-MORROW."
The doctor, taken aback, steps back a couple of
steps, looks at her in astonishment, and says:

SP: "I JUST TOLD YOU THAT I'D MARRY YOU!"
Eve looks at him commiseratingly, smiles a cynical smile, and says:

SP: "YOU JUST TOLD ME YOU WOULD TAKE ME IN
BECAUSE YOU SEE NO WAY TO PREVENT MY BE-
COMING . CHRONIC NEURASTHENIC."
The doctor looks at her, flabbergasted at the
plain way in which she is putting things. She
then goes on and says:

SP: "YOU DON'T WANT ME, BUT YOU'LL TAKE ME
IN AS YOU'D TAKE A PATIENT INTO A HOSPITAL."

The doctor looks at her, tries to speak, stammers, stops, not knowing what to say. Eve then takes a step toward him, smiles commiseratingly, and says:

SP: "YOU DON'T HAVE TO DO THAT. I HAVE LEARNED HOW TO HANDLE MAMA. YOU DON'T HAVE TO WORRY ABOUT MY HEALTH."

The doctor looks at her, surprised at this new Eve, who is in no need of him at all in his professional capacity. Eve looks at him, throws out her arms with gestures of complete victory over all her worries, and says:

SP: "I AM GOING BACK TO NEW YORK, AND I AM GOING TO LIVE."

Eve then turns, starts, goes toward the door and starts to go out. The doctor looks at her, struggles with himself, worries over the fact that he is losing her, goes toward her, and says: "Eve!" She turns, looks at him, and says: "Yes?" He looks at her helplessly, trying to find words to express himself, and then says:

SP: "I CAN'T LET YOU GO LIKE THIS."

Eve looks at him calmly, and asks why. The doctor looks around helplessly, stalls a moment, and then says:

SP: "BECAUSE I LOVE YOU."

Eve looks at him a moment, and then, dropping all her pose, simply overcome with intense relief, she says:

SP: "WELL, THAT'S WHAT I'VE BEEN TRYING TO GET AT."

The doctor rushes over to her, grabs her, takes

her in his arms, looks into her face, and says:

SP: "YOU BOLD-FACED, SHAMELESS LITTLE DAR-
LING."

Then gives her a good kiss, and we FADE OUT.

You will observe that in the scenario there are many lines written in for the actors to speak which never appear on the screen (only those in capitals are shown on the screen). This is to give the cast a chance to say the things they would say in real life under the same circumstances, and so to make the scene entirely natural. The actor speaks all the lines in small type and also those in the capital letters, following the abbreviation "SP," which stands for "Spoken Title."

Contrary to common belief, the actors really speak the words of their lines. There was a day when the hero, kissing the heroine in the final close-up, might say something like "Let's go out and get a cheese sandwich, now that this is over." But just about this time large numbers of lip-readers began to write in to the producers, kicking against this sort of thing. It seems that constant attendance at the movies develops a curious power of following a speech by watching the character's lips. And from that day the slapstick comedians who used to swear so beautifully before the camera and the heroines of the serial thrillers who used to talk about the weather in their big scenes began to speak their proper lines.

CHAPTER IX

INSIDE THE BRAIN OF A MOVIE STAR

"But they have no brains!" someone is sure to say.

That sort of thing is rather cheap cynicism. As a matter of fact, they have plenty of brains, but of their own peculiar sort. A movie actor, like any other type of artist, is an emotional, temperamental creature; but the problem which worries him the most is one of intellect rather than emotion; in short, just how to control the reactions inside that discredited gray matter of his.

Every movie actor—and you, too, if you enter this field—is at one time or another confronted with the perplexing problem of just how much thought he should allow to go into his work; that is, whether his acting should be emotional or intellectual. The question resolves itself into this:

Does an actor feel?

Should he feel?

There are two schools of thought on this seemingly academic but in reality most important subject.

First are those who say that an actor must feel the part he is playing. The greatest actors, they say, have always been those who wore themselves out in an hour's time, because they felt the emotions they portrayed. They tell stories such as that of Mrs. Kendall, who, having lost her own child, electrified an

33

English audience by her portrayal of the bereaved
mother in "East Lynne" to such an extent that women
leaped to their feet in the pit, shouting, "No more, no
more." They point to the fact that the great stars of
the screen and the stage alike are able to simulate the
three reactions which are quite beyond the control of
the will—pallor, blushing, and the sudden perspiration
which comes with great terror or pain. This, they
say, is proof positive that these actors are feeling
every emotion as they enact it.

The second group declares that all this is nonsense
and that if an actor really felt his part he would lose
control of himself, and perhaps actually murder some
other actor in a fight scene. Acting, they say, is an
art wherein the artist, by the use of his intellect, is
able to simulate that which he does not feel—using
his face merely as the painter uses his canvas. The
moment an actor begins to enter into his part, his
acting is either overdone or underdone and the scene
is ruined. The whole trick of it, they add, is to keep
perfectly cool and know exactly what you are doing,
no matter how spectacular the scene.

Still a third school declares that both these views
are wrong, and that acting is neither a matter of
thought nor of emotion, but is purely imitative. An
actor observes his own emotions as he experiences
them in each crisis of his real life, they say, and re-
members them so well that he is afterward able to
reproduce them before the camera.

The truth of it seems to be that all of them are
partly right and partly wrong. The great stars of the
movies to-day, when one is able to draw them out on
the subject, say that when they are acting they are

GLUBING ON A CREPE HAIR MUSTACHE

John Emerson is affixing a villainous mustache to Frank Stockdale. Spirit gum and crepe hair are used.

CALIFORNIA
UNIV. OF

thinking not about one thing but about several things. The brain is divided into different strata, and while one section is thinking about the part, another section is entering into it, while still a third stratum is busying itself with idle speculation about the cameraman and the director.

There are two important secrets, connected with the psychology of screen acting, which every beginner should know, even if he never makes use of them. The first is that of Preparation; the second, that of Auto-Suggestion.

A movie actor or actress is in a more difficult position, so far as the artistry of his work is concerned, than the players of the spoken drama. In the movies the scenes are nearly always taken out of sequence, the first last, the last first, and so forth. For that reason the motion picture stars have great difficulty in working themselves up to the proper "pitch" to play a scene, inasmuch as they have not been through the action which leads up to it.

The movie directors know this, and in most studios try to help them up to this "pitch" by employing small orchestras to play during the important scenes. In nearly every large studio where more than one company is working there are to be heard the faint strains of Sonata Pathetique, where some melancholy scene is being taken, or livelier music for a bit of comedy in another set. Also the directors are always behind the camera to guide their actors with spoken directions as the scene is made. This orchestra business has always seemed to us pure buncombe, but if the director or actor gets any fun out of it, it doesn't do any particular harm.

The wise movie actors of to-day are borrowing these two tricks of Preparation and Auto-Suggestion from their brethren of the stage.

Preparation consists merely of spending a little time before the scene is begun in going over the part, in thinking about it, and in trying really to feel all the emotions of the character in question. This seems a simple matter; but it makes the difference between real acting and routine work. Once an actor has carefully worked out the part for himself he can easily conform to the director's ideas; and once he has let himself feel his part he need waste no emotion upon it when on the "set," for his mimetic powers will reproduce his feelings of an hour before.

Auto-suggestion consists in working oneself up to the part before going before the camera by various expedients. For example, one actor, before playing a part calling for extreme anger, spends some ten minutes in clenching his fists, swearing at the handiest fence post, setting his jaw—and so making himself really angry. It is not hard to reproduce emotion by these tricks of auto-suggestion. Try thinking of something sad—draw your face down—and before long you will be in a very glum mood. That is the way such stars as Norma Talmadge and Mary Pickford produce tears on short notice. Most people think they are tricks of make-up, such as drops of glycerine; as a matter of fact, it is a matter of puckering the face and a few gloomy thoughts.

All this sort of thing sounds very intricate and unnecessary. And yet it is the really practical side of screen acting. The psychology of each actor is different and his manner of preparing for a scene and of enacting it will be different. The important thing is that he be aware that there is such a thing as psychology, and that if he will only understand it as applied to himself he can improve his work as a film player.

CHAPTER X

SALARIES IN THE MOVIES

So much propaganda and press-agentry has been at work during the last few years that no one knows what to believe of the movies. There appears to be a sort of attenuated smoke cloud thrown up about all connected with the artistic, and, more particularly, the financial side of the movies. And naturally the first question to be asked by one who is considering entering this field as a vocation is "What do they pay? Is it all true? Is there money in the movies?"

The leading stars of the screen get anywhere from one thousand to ten thousand dollars a week. There are only two or three stars, however, who get as high as ten thousand. The majority range between one and three thousand.

A few stars are paid a percentage of the profits of the picture. One or two others are paid a lump sum for a picture, rather than a weekly salary, and in one case this lump sum comes to eighty thousand dollars.

A good leading man or leading woman gets four or five hundred dollars a week—some much more. First rate character people, or "heavies," get from three to five hundred a week, or, if called on to play by the day, get anywhere from fifty to a hundred dollars.

The smaller parts bring salaries ranging from fifty to two hundred dollars. "Bits," such as the butler who opens the door, which involve a small bit of individual acting, although really merely atmospheric work, bring ten dollars a day or thereabouts. Extras for the crowd scenes get about five dollars a day.

The salaries of directors range all the way from ten thousand dollars a week, which is the emolument of one great artist, down to the hundred and fifty a week of the fly-by-night concerns. The average director in a large company gets anywhere from five hundred to a thousand dollars a week, especially as at present there is a great shortage of good directors.

Scenario writers are paid according to the type of work they do. If they write original stories they may get from one thousand to twenty thousand dollars for them. Of course, the published works of notable authors or the stage hits of famous playwrights bring more.

Writers doing the adaptations or "continuities" of the stories of others are more often paid by the week. The big scenario writers get salaries ranging up to hundreds of thousands of dollars a year, for this is fast becoming the most important work of the entire industry. The lesser lights seldom receive less than twenty thousand dollars a year.

Cameramen get from one hundred to three hundred dollars a week. Art directors receive several hundred dollars a week, but few companies have as yet realized the necessity of employing specialists in scenic art.

A good five-reel feature picture to-day costs about sixty thousand dollars to produce. If a famous star is employed, the cost of the picture goes to a hundred thousand dollars, or even a hundred and fifty. " 'Way Down East," Griffith's latest production, cost just under a million dollars to produce.

The profits of the picture come out of its run, which may last seven or eight years, and even longer in Europe. A one hundred thousand dollar picture may eventually make half a million dollars for its backers, but, of course, they have a long wait for their money. On the other hand, the risk is stupendous, for the picture may be a flat failure.

One cheering fact, attested by all motion picture magnates, is that, whatever may be the case in other industries, salaries are not going to drop in the movies. On the contrary, the movies are growing bigger and bigger and the demand is greater than ever before. There is money in the movies now, and there will be even more in the next few years.

CHAPTER XI

On the legitimate stage nearly every actor at one time or another writes a play. In the same way, in the movies nearly every actor tries his hand at scenario writing. In fact, many of the most successful playwrights and photodramatists have had stage or screen experience as actors.

For this reason, although this series is designed more for those who wish to act than for those who wish to write—and although we have already one book on "How to Write Photoplays"—nevertheless, a chapter on scenario writing is not out of place.

There is a fine career for any writer in scenario writing if the writer will only take the trouble to study it seriously. There is technique in writing plots and still more technique in adapting those plots to the screen, by writing them into scenario form. Studio experience is of vast benefit to anyone who wishes to write movie stories; and that is where the actor has the advantage over the outsider who tries to write scenarios with no practical knowledge of how movies are really made.

First write your plot into a five hundred or thousand word synopsis, just as you would write it for a magazine. Make it brief and clear. Be sure it is based

41

upon action, mental or physical, and try to give real character to your plot people.

In choosing your story be sure it has the dramatic quality. It must not be rambling; and it must have an element of conflict between opposing factors—a man and a woman, a woman and her Destiny, or simply Good and Evil—which leads up to a crisis in which the matter is fought out and finally settled. Stories which have not these qualities are suitable for novels, perhaps, but not for plays.

It is, as a general rule, inadvisable to try historical stories or stories which require elaborate scenes. Battle stories and stories of the Jules Verne or H. G. Wells type are also difficult to place. The great demand to-day is for sane, wholesome stories of modern American life, wherein character is the paramount interest rather than eccentricities of the plot or camera. Send your story in synopsis form to the scenario editor of the studio which employs the star for whom you think the story is best suited. Send with it a stamped and self-addressed envelope for the return of your script, if it is not suitable for their use. Keep on sending it; don't be discouraged by rejection slips. You may write dozens of stories and then sell the very first one you wrote.

If the studio buys your story it is well to ask for an opportunity to help write the "continuity," or scenario form. This is a highly technical but very well paid task, and one which every screen author should learn. The chance to enter the studio and help work out the scenario of your own story is worth trying for.

Scenarios to-day are more in demand than ever before; but producers are still chary of taking chances

TESTING MAKE-UP AND EXPRESSION

Every make-up must conform to the part. Here the authors, John Emerson and Anita Loos, are helping their director, Victor Fleming, to make a test of Basil Sydney and May Collins, who played the leading roles in "Wife Insurance." The tests are usually taken in some corner of the studio under the best possible lighting conditions.

UNIV. OF
CALIFORNIA

on untried amateurs. The amateur author's greatest success is when he sells his first story. The road is comparatively easy after that.

Original plots for five-reel pictures sell from $1,000 to $20,000, depending upon the reputation of the author and the standing of the company which buys them. Of course, some of the smaller companies pay less than this, and two and three reel features sell for less.

Published stories and novels, and plays which have had a run, bring enormous prices. Griffith recently paid $150,000 for the film rights on a play. Fifty and seventy thousand dollars are frequently paid for similar plot material, but that is because of the advertising value in the names of the plays or books, or the reputation of the writers, which assures the producers that the story is almost sure to make a good photoplay.

The highest paid workers in the movies to-day are the continuity writers, who put the stories into scenario form and write the "titles" or written inserts. The income of some of these writers runs into hundreds of thousands of dollars a year. It is extraordinarily interesting work and well worth while learning; but unfortunately the technical training for this sort of thing takes as much time as the training necessary to enter any other profession.

Scenario writing does not require great genius. It does require a dramatic insight and certain amount of training. It is the latter factor that most amateurs overlook. If you are to write scenarios, you must take your work as seriously as you would if you were trying to write music or paint pictures.

CHAPTER XII

HOW OTHERS HAVE DONE IT

THE histories of the movie celebrities are as picturesque as the story of their industry. Nearly all of them have risen from the ranks. Few of them, in the days when the motion picture was classed as a freak novelty, expected the present amazing expansion of the industry; still fewer had any conception of their own latent talents in photodramatic art.

But characteristics which they all had in common were determination to succeed in their profession, a modest faith in its future, and a desire to learn the business from the ground up.

It is a curious fact that many of the directors of to-day were once automobile mechanics. This is not because automobile mechanics are as a class better fitted for such work, but because, in the old days of 1907 and 1908 and 1909, when everything started, they had a singular opportunity to apprentice themselves to the profession.

In those days companies worked almost entirely out of doors, and the cameraman transported his paraphernalia in an automobile. The driver of the automobile would usually assist the cameraman in "setting up"; a friendship would spring up between them; presently the driver would be assistant cameraman, then chief cameraman, and finally director. Of course,

44

directors have been recruited from every profession and every class—actors, authors, professors, newspaper men, scene carpenters, artists—for the dramatic gift is not confined to any class. What a man's profession was before he entered the movies has nothing to do with his career thereafter; he has to learn everything all over again, and a very good actor, with years of studio experience, may make a very poor director, whereas an unsuccessful tinsmith might suddenly rise to the top by virtue of an innate gift for this type of work.

The scenario writers of to-day have also grown up with the business. Some were newspaper men who broke into the game as press-agents; some were actors; others were directors. Recently a large number of professional playwrights, novelists and authors with magazine experience have entered the movies to learn scenario writing, but this is a new development.

The writers of this series have been asked to tell how they themselves broke into the scenario offices. Unlike the others, our own story has nothing picturesque about it. Miss Loos was born and bred in a California town; she was the daughter of a newspaper proprietor and inherited that fatal desire to write. At the age of fourteen she sent her first scenario to Griffith; for a miracle, it was accepted—but, of course, it was easy to sell stories in those days, when scenario writing was almost unheard of outside of California. Soon after this she paid a personal visit to the Griffith studios and became the youngest scenario editor in the world, turning out a new story about every six weeks. Some six years ago Mr. Emerson left his post as producer for Frohman on the legitimate stage and went to Hollywood to keep an eye on the filming of one of his own plays which was being adapted from the "speakies." He decided to make the movies a permanent profession, and with this in mind worked as an actor about the Griffith studios to learn the rudiments of the game. Some months after this he was allowed to direct his first picture; and at this time he met Miss Loos, who was to write the scenario. After that they collaborated in the Doug' Fairbanks' pictures—and that's that.

Most of the present-day movie actors and actresses gained their experience as extras, although a few have first made their success on the legitimate stage and then stepped directly into film stardom. Doug' Fairbanks was one of the latter, and so was Mary Pickford. Charley Chaplin and Wallace Reid, on the other hand, have done little of note outside of the movies.

Both Norma Talmadge and Constance Talmadge rose from the ranks. They took small parts in the old Vitagraph pictures; but their extraordinary beauty and talent was immediately recognized by the directors, and they were permitted to try bits, then parts, and finally leads. Norma Talmadge went in for the more emotional rôles, while Constance developed her ability as a comedienne. Within six years they have attained to position of leadership in their respective fields.

D. W. Griffith himself was once an extra. He was a good extra, too, according to some of his former employers who now work under him in his great studios at Mamaroneck, Conn. But he had all manner of queer ideas as to how pictures should be acted, and directed and photographed. For example, he thought that more effective scenes might be made, at times, by photographing actors "close up," cutting off their legs and arms with the frame of the picture and showing only their faces many times enlarged; also he had a theory that one might heighten the dramatic suspense by "cutting back" from one scene to another, instead of following one line of action in a monotonous sequence through an entire photoplay. The directors and actors and cameramen of those days, who would no sooner have thought of taking a character's picture from the bust up than of taking the picture upside down, were nevertheless interested in this eccentric chap, and even asked his advice from time to time. Finally, the eccentric extra got his chance as a director to try out a few of these radical theories. His "The Birth of a Nation" changed the entire technique of the movies.

Many noted directors received their training in directing plays for the legitimate stage, as, for example, Hugh Ford. Others, like Marshall Neilan, or Allan Dwan, came in from outside professions. Victor Fleming, formerly director for Douglas Fairbanks and Constance Talmadge, was one of the latter. His first success, many years ago, was as an automobile designer, but his interest always lay with the theater; he resigned his post with the automobile company at about the age when most young men are seeking their first jobs, and decided to learn the business of making movies. The same creative faculty which made his automobile designs distinctive in the old days manifested itself in his pictures last

year, "The Mollycoddle" and "When the Clouds Roll
By."

There are a million ways to break into the movies.
No one can imitate the career of another. Don't read
other people's biographies; go out and make one for
yourself.

CHAPTER XIII

AMATEUR theatrical clubs, theater guilds, and the like, have done much to make the modern drama the great art that it is. But because of the overwhelming expense heretofore attached to the making of movies there have been no attempts at any similar activities in the films. The movies have never had the advantage of the experiments of amateur societies.

To-day, however, the making of movies by amateurs is a distinct possibility. The possibilities of making a motion picture at comparatively little expense were first drawn to public attention five years ago when two young men, both of whom have become well-known directors, made a saleable photoplay in their own back yard. These boys had many theories about what a movie should and should not be, but they could never find a company willing to give their theories a trial. Finally they hit upon the original expedient of buying their own camera and making a picture in which nearly all the actors were children and which therefore cost very little money. Nearly all the scenes were exteriors, so that practically no scenery was required. The picture was most original and in spite of their technical shortcomings, they found a fairly profitable sale.

49

If you desire to write, direct or act in the pictures, you can have no better experience than trying to make a picture of your own, even if at first you are not very successful.

The great initial expense for this sort of thing is, of course, the outlay required to buy a camera. In most towns of any size there are now professional movie cameramen who work for the news reel companies and who may be hired for a comparatively small sum. If, however, you desire to make your photoplay an entirely amateur affair, you can buy a usable second-hand camera for outdoor work for as low as a hundred dollars.

Some one of your associates must make it his business to learn to run this camera with sufficient skill to insure that your film will not be wasted.

The next important outlay is that of the film itself. Film costs about eleven or twelve cents a foot when developed and printed. Therefore, the cost of production depends largely upon the length of your picture. For a first attempt we should advise you to keep your photoplay within 2,000 feet, or two reels.

Start by writing a simple story into a scenario with as many exterior scenes as possible. The necessary interiors, such as rooms or hallways, may be built by your own amateurs, outdoors, as they are often built in California, so that no lights will be necessary. You can paint your own subtitle cards—the written inserts—and film them yourself.

It is not necessary to make the scenes in their natural sequence. After the picture is finished and developed, however, someone must assemble and cut it.

MAKING A "CLOSE-UP"

Sun reflectors, consisting of silvered canvas screens, are used to lighten the shadows, which are apt to make the cheeks seem hollow. The actors are Basil Sydney and May Collins.

UNIV. OF
CALIFORNIA

This means that you must rent the use of the projection machine at your local theater for a few mornings, and get the local operator to help you splice and cement the film together in its correct order of long shots and close-ups. There is no rule for this work except that of practical values on the screen. Just run your bits of film through the projection machine and stick them together the way they look best. It is a matter of artistic perception rather than any set rule.

If your scenario calls for an outdoor picture—for example, a cowboy story—which does not require costumes, you should be able to make it for a thousand dollars, provided your amateur actors, and amateur cameramen, and amateur authors are working for nothing. There are mighty few amateur theatricals of any pretention whatsoever which do not cost as much as this, and you should be able to take in a good profit if your picture is exploited in your local theaters.

As a matter of fact, pictures have not always been produced on the scale that they are to-day. Ten years ago feature pictures cost from $5,000 to $7,000 to make, and in those days film and cameras were much more expensive. The producers simply made outdoor pictures which required no lights or scenery, and saved on the salaries of actors and directors, which have multiplied twenty times since then. To-day the average feature picture costs from $50,000 to $150,000 to produce. Griffith's " 'Way Down East" cost nearly a million to produce. That is because the salaries of actors, directors and authors have risen so enormously.

But there is no reason why an amateur company in which the cost of salaries is completely eliminated cannot make their own picture at a minimum expense. If you want to break into the movies, here is a way to do it, right in your own home town.

INTRODUCTORY NOTE TO PART II

WHETHER you desire to break into the movies as writer, actor or director, your most important consideration will be the scenario. In the scenario you will find all the elements of the photoplay; everything is built upon that as a foundation. The actor or director who sincerely desires to do good work studies his script assiduously. The ambitious writer analyzes not only his own photoplays, but those of other people.

It is exceedingly difficult to talk technique to anyone who has never read a scenario. For this reason we have incorporated a "continuity" in this book. It is the dramatic form of a screen story which we have made as a special production. The titles, which are the written inserts to be flashed on the screen, are in capital letters. The inserts refer to such articles as letters, telegrams, pictures, and the like, which may be shown in close-up. The "iris" is the broadening or narrowing of the frame of the picture to open or close a scene, or to emphasize some particular object which is "irised" upon. The "fade" effects are used very much as the curtain of the legitimate stage is used to open and close scenes. The abbreviation "Sp" means "Speech," indicating that the title which follows is to be spoken by the actor. Some of the quoted lines—the ones not set off in capitals—are not shown on the screen, but are merely given as a guide for the players.

Most of the directions concerning the scenes are also given in capital letters. "EXTERIOR," or the abbreviated "EXT.," for example, refers to a scene outdoors, while "INTERIOR" or "INT.," is an indoor scene. The terms "LONG SHOT" and "CLOSE-UP" refer to the distance at which the camera is placed from the scene.

"Red Hot Romance" is played as a romantic melodrama, but is intended as a satire upon this very type of story, with its incredibly heroic hero, its American girl, its marines-to-the-rescue and all the rest of it. Basil Sydney and May Collins played the parts of Roland and Rosalie, and Victor Fleming was the director.

RED HOT ROMANCE

T: IT'S BAD ENOUGH FOR SOME TO BOSS THE REST OF US WHILE THEY ARE ALIVE, BUT THE LIMIT IS REACHED WHEN THEY WANT TO KEEP RIGHT ON AFTER THEY HAVE CASHED IN.

T: FOR INSTANCE, THERE WAS OLD HARDER N. STONE, THE VICE-PRESIDENT OF THE BRITISH-AMERICAN INSURANCE CO.

1. LIBRARY, STONE HOME IN WASHINGTON. (Fade in.) Harder N. Stone, an old skinflint, is seated at his desk writing.

INSERT—Stone's hand writing the following:

"I, Harder N. Stone, of Washington, D. C., hereby direct that, should I die before my son, Roland Stone, he is to receive from my estate the sum of $50.00 per week and the use of my residence in Washington, D. C., until his twenty-fifth birthday."

Stone sits back and regards what he has been writing, smiles smugly, and then continues writing.

INSERT—Stone's hand writing the following:

"On his twenty-fifth birthday, provided he has lived according to instructions herein set down, my son, Roland Stone, is to receive his inheritance at the hands of my chosen executor, Lord Howe-Greene, of London, President of the British-American Insurance Co."

Stone sits back and reads over what he has written and is highly pleased. He then rings for a servant and presently Briggs enters. He is a little English butler, who has been in the family for years. Stone turns to him and tells him that he has just been making out his will. Briggs is properly impressed and Stone says to him:

SP: "BRIGGS, I HAVE PROVIDED IN MY WILL

55

THAT IF I DIE BEFORE MY SON YOU ARE
TO STAY ON WITH HIM AS LONG AS YOU
LIVE."
Briggs is highly pleased, thanks him, Stone
dismisses him, goes on writing. (Fade out.)
THE OLD BOY DID DIE, AS HE DE-
SERVED TO, AND LEFT HIS SON AND
HEIR, ROLAND STONE, WITH NOTHING
TO DO BUT LIVE ON $50.00 PER WEEK.

2.   ROLAND'S BEDROOM. (Fade in.) He is
lolling in bed in pajamas and dressing gown,
smoking a cigarette and opening a stack of bills
and reading them.

INSERT—top bill—tailor's bill with a balance from the
month before and about $275.00 for this month
with a note in heavy letters "PLEASE REMIT."
This one is turned over, and the second one is
from a club with a statement "You have this day
been posted for $179.00 and your credit is hereby
suspended until same is paid." This bill is turned
over and the third bill is from a florist's for $950.00
worth of flowers sent to Miss Rosalie Bird and
has a note reading: "Impossible for us to fill
any more orders until these bills are paid."

Roland puts down the bills in disgust, not
looking further, as he knows they're all alike.

Briggs, the butler, now enters and takes up
the breakfast tray which is lying on the bed
opposite beside Roland. Roland looks up to him,
then looks at the bills, and says:

SP: "HOW DO YOU EXPECT ME TO PAY
THESE BILLS ON $50.00 A WEEK?"

Briggs shrugs his shoulders as though he
had nothing to do with it, and suggests that
Roland's bills are too big. He then leaves. Roland looks after him, disgusted, runs through a
few more bills, throws them on the floor and at
this juncture, Tom, Roland's valet, a big husky
negro with a child-like, innocent smile, enters the
room with letters, goes to Roland and hands him
the letters. Roland looks at them and sees they
are more bills, puts them down. Tom picks up
others from floor and gives them to Roland, much
to his disgust. He looks up to Tom and says:

SP: "YOU'RE A FINE 'SECRETARY'! WHAT DO I PAY YOU FOR?"

Tom looks up at him, round-eyed and smiles and says:

SP: "YOU DON'T."

This is a poser for Roland for a moment, he finally regains his composure and says:

SP: "WELL, I AM GOING TO WHEN I GET MY INHERITANCE NEXT APRIL."

Tom nods his head quizzically as he has heard this many times before. Roland then picks up the bills, runs through them again and says:

SP: "THE QUESTION NOW IS—HOW ARE WE GOING TO LIVE UNTIL APRIL?"

He sighs, reaches over to a table which has a little calendar on it, picks up the calendar, sees that it is the 13th of January, and runs through the pages very dubiously. He finally looks up at Tom, shows him how many days they have to live through on the calendar, and says:

SP: "I HAVEN'T A NICKEL AND I CAN'T BORROW ANYTHING NOW. HOW ARE WE GOING TO LIVE UNTIL APRIL?"

Tom looks about very dubiously. Finally he gets an idea, he looks from one object of furniture to another, and his idea grows until he is fairly beaming and he says:

SP: "THEY'S A MIGHTY LOT OF HOCKABLE STUFF AROUND HEAH, BOSS!"

He indicates the things around the room, and Roland is delighted with the idea. He picks up the bunch of bills, looks at the top one.

INSERT—TAILOR'S BILL.

Roland then looks around for something to pay that with and his eye falls upon an antique vase. He jumps out of bed, takes the vase and hands it to Tom together with the tailor's bill, saying that that will pay for that. Roland looks at the next bill.

INSERT—BILL FROM CLUB.

Roland then takes a couple of ornaments from the mantel, gives them to Tom together with the club bill saying that they will pay for that. Roland then looks at the next bill.

INSERT—FLORIST'S BILL.
>Roland then takes a picture from the wall, leaving a discolored place behind it, saying that will pay for that. He then thinks a moment and picks up a little antique clock and hands it to Tom, saying:

SP: "AND BUY HER SOME ORCHIDS WITH THIS."
>Tom grins, goes out loaded down with all the junk. Roland looks after him, very pleased with himself, and, probably thinking of his girl and the orchids, smiles, and fade out.

T: INDICATING THAT IT'S TEA TIME.

3.   EXTERIOR COLONEL BIRD'S HOUSE. (Fade in.)
>Roland comes down the street with a bunch of orchids in his hand and goes up and rings the bell.

T: COLONEL BIRD, OF VIRGINIA, WHO HAS BEEN HANGING AROUND WASHINGTON FOR THIRTY-FIVE YEARS, WAITING FOR A JOB WHICH WAS FIRST PROMISED HIM BY PRESIDENT CLEVELAND.

4   PARLOR, COLONEL BIRD'S HOUSE. Colonel Bird, seated at a desk, very busily reading several large law books and making notes, trying to "kid" himself into believing that he is busy. A colored mammy presently shows in Roland, who greets the Colonel very effusively. The Colonel asks Roland to sit down, which he does. The servant exits. The Colonel, not being very greatly impressed with Roland, excuses himself and goes on with his work, explaining that he has some very important matters on hand. Roland looks at him, smiles to himself, then looks out expectantly toward the hall.

T: THE COLONEL'S DAUGHTER, ROSALIE, THE LADY OF THE ORCHIDS.

5.   HALLWAY, COLONEL'S HOUSE. Rosalie comes down the stairs and enters the parlor.

6.   PARLOR, COLONEL'S HOUSE. Rosalie rushes over, greets Roland. The Colonel rises until Roland and the girl are seated on a sofa, when he sits and goes on with his

work. Roland gives Rosalie the orchids. Rosalie thanks him, but says:

SP: "ROLAND, YOU SHOULDN'T BUY OR-CHID'S EVERY DAY."

She then points around to different vases in the room, all of which are full of orchids. She holds on to the orchids and gives Roland a little lecture on economy, telling him he has no business to spend his money so foolishly. And Roland says he thought she liked orchids. She says she does and he's a dear sweet boy to bring them, but he sees she is not pleased and is correspondingly depressed.

7. EXTERIOR COLONEL'S BIRD'S HOUSE. A low rakish roadster drives up and out of it gets Jim Conwell. He has a small sized package in his hand.

CLOSE UP—And he runs up and rings the bell.

T: JIM CONWELL IS ONE OF THAT BROTH-ERHOOD OF DIPLOMATIC HANGERS-ON WHO MAKE A SHADY LIVELIHOOD BY DOING THE DIRTY WORK OF THE VARI-OUS WASHINGTON EMBASSIES.

8. EXT. COLONEL BIRD'S PORCH. The col-ored mammy opens the door, lets in Conwell, takes his hat and coat and shows him into the parlor.

9. PARLOR COLONEL BIRD'S HOUSE. The colored mammy shows Conwell in, the old Colonel jumps up from his desk, and greets him very enthusiastically. His manner toward Con-well is very different from his manner toward Roland. Rosalie then greets Conwell very sweetly but with reserve and Roland, giving him a dirty look, greets him as coldly as possible. The old Colonel now gives up his work to join the group. Conwell holds out his little package toward Rosalie and says:

SP: "HERE'S A LITTLE THING I PICKED UP IN AN ANTIQUE SHOP. I THOUGHT YOU'D LIKE IT."

Rosalie puts down her orchids in Roland's chair. She then takes the package, opens it up and takes out Roland's clock. She lets out a cry of surprise and delight, then turns to Conwell and says:

SP: "IT'S LOVELY! I'VE ALWAYS WANTED A CLOCK LIKE THAT."

Roland looks at this, open-mouthed and in absolute astonishment, sits down in his chair, smashing the orchids. Rosalie then shows the clock to the old Colonel and the two of them rave over it, forgetting the existence of Roland, who finally comes to sufficiently to see that he's sitting on something, gets up and picks up the mashed orchids, looks at them disgustedly. The clock is finally put in place on the mantel and Rosalie comes back and joins Roland, who stands looking ruefully at the flowers in his hand. He dolefully shows them to her, and she, seeing he is hurt, comforts him, telling him he's a dear boy and she loves the orchids. She takes them from him and tenderly straightens them out, but Roland is still in the dumps. Conwell is now throwing a lot of "bull" at the old Colonel, saying:

SP: "I JUST SAID TO THE SECRETARY OF STATE: 'YOU'RE NOT LOOKING VERY WELL, ELIHU, I WISH YOU'D LET MY OLD FRIEND, COLONEL BIRD, TAKE SOME OF THE WORK OFF YOUR HANDS.'"

He goes on spouting and the old Colonel fairly eats it up. Finally, Roland, unhappy and jealous and disgusted at Conwell, gets up and tells Rosalie he has to go. Rosalie begs him to stay in her sweetest manner, but Roland takes another look at Conwell, says no, he's got to go, says good-by to Rosalie and says good-by to the Colonel and Conwell, and leaves.

STREET EXT. COL. BIRD'S HOUSE.—Roland comes out and goes dolefully down the street. (Fade out.)

HALLWAY ROLAND'S HOUSE. Roland enters, disheartened. Hangs up hat and coat and stick and goes slowly into library.

10.   LIBRARY ROLAND'S HOUSE. (Fade in.) Tom is fussing about the room. Roland enters

the room, terribly depressed and upset and starts
to tell Tom about the scene that just took
place. He goes on talking about Conwell and
finally says:

SP: "THE OLD MAN STANDS FOR ALL OF
CONWELL'S BUNK AND THINKS HE'S
GREAT."

Tom is very sympathetic and tells Roland he
ought to settle the matter. Roland agrees with
him, pounds on the table, and says:

SP: "I THINK THE TIME HAS COME WHEN
I OUGHT TO TELL ROSALIE I LOVE
HER!"

Tom agrees with him, says that's absolutely
right. Roland says he knows it's right—the only
thing to do is to come to an understanding right
away. He then goes over to the telephone and
calls a number, and while he is waiting for the
number, he goes on talking to Tom, telling him
just how he is going to settle things and Tom
encourages him.

11. HALLWAY COLONEL BIRD'S HOUSE.
Rosalie comes down the hall to the telephone
and answers it.

12. LIBRARY ROLAND'S HOUSE. Roland is
still talking to Tom, telling him how he's going
to lay down the law when he suddenly hears
Rosalie's voice over the 'phone. All his belliger-
ency oozes out. He smiles and stammers foolishly and gulps and tries to get his courage up
as if he were going to lay matters right before
her and finally weakens and comes out with

SP: "HOW ARE YOU?"

13. HALLWAY COLONEL BIRD'S HOUSE.
Rosalie, wondering what the devil he's asking
her that for when he just left her, frowns quizzically and says that she's feeling all right.

14. LIBRARY ROLAND'S HOUSE. Roland goes
on talking through the 'phone in a stammering
embarrassed sort of way, and Tom keeps telling
him to go on and tell her what he said he was
going to. Roland tries to motion to Tom and
he goes on stammering and stuttering.

15. HALLWAY COLONEL BIRD'S HOUSE.

Rosalie still very quizzically listening to Roland. She finally asks him what is the matter with him.

16. LIBRARY ROLAND'S HOUSE. Roland stammering into the 'phone. Finally Tom, utterly disgusted, comes over to the 'phone and yells in it:

SP: "HE'S TRYING TO ASK YOU TO MARRY HIM, MISS ROSALIE! WILL YOU?"

Roland turns angrily to Tom, still holding the receiver to his ear, and starts to berate Tom soundly, when he suddenly hears something in the telephone which stops him. He listens, overcome with wonderment and finally says:

SP: "SAY THAT AGAIN!"

17. HALLWAY COLONEL BIRD'S HOUSE. Rosalie at the 'phone, laughing, says:

SP: "YES. OF COURSE I WILL!"

18. LIBRARY ROLAND'S HOUSE. Roland can hardly believe his ears, makes her reiterate it, then turns to Tom in great glee and says:

SP: "IT'S ALL RIGHT. SHE SAYS YES."

He then turns back to the 'phone and asks Rosalie if she really means it. While he is talking to Rosalie, Tom goes over to a heavy couch, pulls it out toward the hall. Roland still at the 'phone talking, turns and asks Tom what he is doing. Tom still pulling the couch says:

SP: "AH'M GOING TO BUY YOU A ENGAGEMENT RING."

Roland smiles and nods, and suddenly thinks of the clock episode, stops Tom, tells him to wait a minute, then turns toward the telephone and says:

SP: "WHAT WOULD YOU RATHER HAVE—A RING OR A SOFA?"

19. HALLWAY COLONEL BIRD'S HOUSE. Rosalie listening at the 'phone is utterly dumbfounded at this odd request, she asks him to repeat it, then finally still puzzled, says:

SP: "WHY, A RING, OF COURSE! YOU SILLY BOY!"

20. LIBRARY ROLAND'S HOUSE. Roland listening at the 'phone, hears Rosalie wants the ring, turns to Tom and tells him to go on and hock

the sofa. He then turns to Rosalie, starts in to talk to her ecstatically over the 'phone, smiling, as we fade out.

T: THAT NIGHT AT THE HANGOUT OF THE FRINGE OF THE DIPLOMATIC SET.

21. A WOP RESTAURANT. (Fade in.) This is a typical $1.35 Table d'Hote joint. Seated at the various tables are many diplomatic hangers-on, all of them crooked and all looking out for the main chance. Among them is a Mexican, a Frenchman, an Englishman, a German, a Russian, an Italian, a Chinaman, a Jap, a Bulgarian, a Hindoo and their women—perhaps three or four Americans, but the atmosphere is generally foreign, the waiters being Wops.

Seated at one table is Conwell alone. He is eating spaghetti and looking very sourly about.

T: ENRICO DE CASTANET OF BUNKONIA.

Enrico is seated at a table talking to a very attractive vamp type of a woman.

T: HIS LADY FRIEND (THE INTERNATIONAL VAMP AND SPY), COUNTESS PULLOFF DE PLOTZ.

The Countess is listening very intently to Enrico. Enrico goes on talking very earnestly, and finally says:

SP: "YOU SEE, WE MUST HAVE A MAN WHO CAN BE BOUGHT BODY AND SOUL."

The Countess agrees with him, and perhaps suggests somebody, whom Enrico says would never do. The Countess starts thinking again, and, as she does, her eyes wander over the room and she sees Conwell, who has just gotten up, paid his bill and given the waiter a very small tip, at which the waiter shows his disgust. Conwell then turns to leaves the restaurant, starts down toward Enrico and the Countess. The Countess sees him, has a sudden idea that he would be fine for the job and points him out to Enrico. At this moment, Conwell has stopped to talk to someone at one of the tables, Enrico looks him over from head to foot, asks the Countess if she is sure he can be handled; she assures him he can.

SP: "HE WORKED FOR THE SHIPPING BOARD."

Enrico agrees that he looks like a good bet, and just at this moment Conwell comes past the table, sees the Countess motion to him. He comes over to the table, Enrico rises and the Countess introduces him saying:

SP: "SENOR DE CASTANET IS MINISTER OF WAR OF BUNKONIA."

Conwell is mildly interested in this fact. Enrico then asks Conwell to sit down, so he takes a seat, and the Countess then begins to get very confidential. She looks around to see that no one is looking, then getting their three heads together, she says in whispered tones:

SP: "WE ARE ENGINEERING A LITTLE REVOLUTION DOWN IN BUNKONIA."

'Conwell is a little more interested now. He pricks up his ears a bit and casually glances around to make sure no one is overhearing, then looks to De Castanet for some information, and De Castanet, with a quick glance around says to Conwell:

SP: "THE AMERICAN CONSUL HAS RESIGNED AND A NEW ONE IS TO BE APPOINTED NEXT MONTH." •

Conwell is still more interested, asks Enrico where do I come in? Enrico says, indicating Madame:

SP: "I AM HERE TO SEE THAT THE 'RIGHT' MAN IS APPOINTED."

Conwell says "Oh ho," he sees and looks at the Countess, who nods her approval. He then asks her where he comes in. With more mysterious looks, they get their heads very closely together, and the Countess says:

SP: "WHAT'S THE MATTER WITH YOU FOR CONSUL? THE PICKINGS ARE GOING TO BE FINE FOR THE 'RIGHT MAN.'"

Conwell considers a moment, smiles quizzically and shakes his head and says:

SP: "NO, I'M IN WRONG—THE SENATE WOULDN'T CONFIRM ME."

The Countess tries to argue with him but he

is obdurate and says there's no chance for him,
but as they are talking he is suddenly struck
with a brilliant idea. He says, "Wait a minute."
They all wait and finally he speaks and says:

SP: "I'VE GOT JUST THE MAN FOR YOU!"
They are all attention and eager to know who
it is. He indicates that this must be very much
on the quiet and then says:

SP: "OLD COLONEL BIRD—FINE RECORD—
EASY TO HANDLE—BEEN WAITING
THIRTY-FIVE YEARS FOR A JOB."
The Countess indicates that she knows old
Bird and tells Enrico that he is ideal, that they
couldn't do better. Enrico asks if he can be
handled when the time comes. Conwell swells
up and tells him to leave that to him. It's
the easiest thing in the world. Enrico turns to
Madame, who backs up Conwell and Enrico is
then satisfied. Conwell then speaks up and
says:

SP: "I'LL GO ALONG AS SECRETARY AND
KEEP MY EYE ON THE OLD BOY."
They both express their approval of that, and
indicate that he will get part of the swag. The
Countess leans over and says rather tauntingly:

SP: "I SUPPOSE THE OLD BOY'S DAUGHTER
WILL GO ALONG, TOO!"
Conwell says he bets she will and winks the
other eye. The Countess laughs and Enrico
smiles, interested at the idea of a romance. He
and the Countess exchange glances. Conwell
then says:

SP: "REMEMBER—MUM'S THE WORD UNTIL
AFTER THE APPOINTMENT IS MADE."
They all agree to that and put their heads
together and go on with their scheming. (Fade
out.)

T: AND SO IT CAME TO PASS——

22.   PARLOR COLONEL BIRD'S HOUSE. (Fade
in.) An old trunk in the middle of the floor
and the Colonel and mammy are packing in his
books, papers, etc. The Colonel all full of business and very busy. Rosalie is helping, but is
very sad over the matter.

23. EXTERIOR COLONEL BIRD'S HOUSE.
Roland rushes down the street with a newspaper
in his hand, runs up the steps and rings the
bell.

24. PARLOR COLONEL BIRD'S HOUSE. Rosalie looks up quickly, thinking that this must be
Roland. Mammy starts for the door but Rosalie
tells her she will answer the bell, and she runs
out into hall.

25. HALLWAY COLONEL BIRD'S HOUSE.
Rosalie runs to the door and opens it.

26. EXTERIOR COLONEL BIRD'S HOUSE.
Rosalie opens the door, and Roland rushes in.

27. HALLWAY COLONEL BIRD'S HOUSE.
Roland, full of excitement, grabs Rosalie, shows
her the article in the newspaper.

INSERT—Article in newspaper stating that Colonel Bird
has been appointed Consul of Bunkonia and that
he is to leave for there immediately with his
daughter and his Secretary, James Conwell.

Roland asks Rosalie if this is true. Rosalie
nods her head sadly, says that it is and

SP: "I DIDN'T KNOW A THING ABOUT IT
MYSELF UNTIL THIS MORNING."

Roland protests that she can't go away and
leave him, and Rosalie asks what she can do
and says that her father has waited for this all
his life and insists on taking her along. Roland
asks where her father is, she points into parlor,
and Roland tells her that he will see about
whether she will be taken away or not, and
full of worry, rushes into the parlor followed
by Rosalie.

28. PARLOR COLONEL BIRD'S HOUSE.
Colonel Bird is helping mammy pack and Roland
rushes in followed by Rosalie. He goes to the
Colonel and protests against taking his fiancée
away from him. He puts his arm around Rosalie
and says that he wants to marry her now and
keep her. The Colonel can't see this at all, and
says:

SP: "IF YOU MARRY NOW, HOW ARE YOU
GOING TO SUPPORT HER?"

Rosalie turns to Roland and says that is the

trouble—that her father won't let her stay there and marry him because he can't support her. Roland then turns to the Colonel and says:

SP: "BUT, COLONEL, IN ANOTHER MONTH EVERYTHING WILL BE ALL RIGHT!"

Rosalie seconds the motion and tries to persuade her father that everything will be all right, but her father shakes his head, looks grimly at Roland and says:

SP: "THAT'S WHAT CLEVELAND SAID TO ME IN '89."

Roland looks discouraged and realizes that he is up against a hard proposition in the old Colonel, but tries to explain that if they can just struggle along for a month he will have millions, but the Colonel says:

SP: "WHEN YOU HAVE YOUR INHERITANCE RIGHT IN YOUR HAND, COME DOWN TO BUNKONIA AND GET HER."

Roland, much discouraged, still tries to argue with the old boy, but he cuts him off and goes on about his work. Roland then turns to Rosalie, who by this time is in tears. At the sight of Rosalie's tears, Roland forgets his own disappointment, and putting his arm around her, leads her off to a secluded corner out of sight of the old Colonel, seats her and tries to comfort her, putting his arm around her and saying:

SP: "THE FIRST OF APRIL IS MY BIRTHDAY. I GET MY INHERITANCE THAT DAY AND I'LL START AT ONCE FOR BUNKONIA."

At once Rosalie looks up at him with her eyes full of tears and smiles wanly. Roland takes her hand, wipes away her tears, kisses her and says:

SP: "I'LL SEND YOU A CABLE EVERY DAY!"

At this Rosalie is greatly cheered up, she looks and says: "Will you, dear?" and he assures her that he will and again kisses her. (Fade out.)

T: THE AMERICAN CABLE COMPANY DID WELL THAT MONTH BUT LOOK WHAT HAPPENED TO ROLAND'S HOUSE.

29.   HALLWAY ROLAND'S HOUSE. (Fade in.)

View of hall without a piece of furniture, bric-a-brac or pictures. (Dissolve out.)

30. LIBRARY ROLAND'S HOUSE. (Dissolve in.) View of Library absolutely bare. (Dissolve out.)

31. ROLAND'S BEDROOM. (Dissolve in.) Bedroom has nothing in it but one couch, one chair and a soap box on which are Roland's mirror and toilet articles.

Roland is asleep on the couch. Presently Briggs enters, looks about at the devastated room, then shaking his head over the laziness of his master, goes over, wakes Roland up and says:

SP: "I WISH YOU A HAPPY BIRTHDAY, SIR."

Roland wakes up, looks at him, rubs his eyes, realizes that his probation is over. Tom enters smiling with a telegram in his hand which he gives to Roland who opens it and reads:

INSERT—TELEGRAM.

New York, March 31, 1920. "Arrive Washington four-forty to-morrow, April first, to deliver inheritance. HOWE-GREENE."

Roland jumps out of bed, goes over and claps Briggs on the back and shakes hands with him—then shakes hands with Tom. Then makes Briggs and Tom shake hands. Tells them both he's going to have loads of money and they will be paid. Roland then goes over to his soap box on which is a calendar. He looks at page marked "March 31." Tears it off and looks at page marked "April 1."

He tears off the page with a flourish which reads March 31st, turns it over, and, sitting on the floor, writes on the back of it. Tom in the meantime sends Briggs for his breakfast and gets out Roland's clothes, brushing them with great gusto. Roland finishes writing and reads what he has written.

INSERT—WHAT ROLAND IS WRITING.

"Miss Rosalie Bird, Santo Grafto, Bunkonia. At last the great day is here. Lord Howe-Greene arrives to-day with my inheritance. Leave for Bunkonia to-morrow to claim you as my bride. Roland."

He reads it and tells Tom to send it. Tom takes the message. Scratches his head and looks around the room for something to hock. Roland wants to know why he's hesitating, and he tells him. Roland then says:

SP: "TAKE THE COUCH!"

Tom looks at the couch dubiously, then looks at Roland and says: "Where are you going to sleep to-night?" Roland, in an extravagant manner and with a grand flourish, tells him to take it away.

SP: "I WON'T BE ABLE TO SLEEP TO-NIGHT ANYWAY!"

Tom goes over, picks up the couch and starts out of the room with it. At the door, Roland stops him, picks up the one remaining chair, hands it over to him and says:

SP: "CABLE HER SOME ROSES WITH THIS!"

Tom takes the chair, starts for the door when he suddenly thinks of the fact that Lord Howe-Greene is due that morning, so he stops, turns to Roland and says:

SP: WHAT DAT LORD HOWE-GREENE TO SIT ON WHEN HE COMES?"

Roland says that's right, so he leaves the chair and starts out with the couch. Briggs in the meantime has entered with Roland's breakfast. Puts breakfast on soap box. Roland tells him to put the chair down in the hall. Briggs doleful. Roland slaps him on the back—tells him to cheer up. Briggs goes out shaking his head and Roland sits on chair and starts his breakfast all smiles. (Fade out.)

T: THE NEW MILLIONAIRE.

32. FRONT OF ROLAND'S HOUSE. (Fade in.) Roland's taxi drives up and stops, followed by Tom's. Roland and Lord Howe-Greene with portfolio get out. Tom also gets out with bags. Howe-Greene starts up walk. Tom stops Roland and shows him three cents—all he has and whispers to him, saying:

SP: "HOW DO I PAY THE TAXI?"

Roland signifying that he can't be annoyed with such little things, says grandiloquently:

SP: "TELL THEM TO WAIT!"
He follows Lord Howe-Greene up the walk while Tom goes to the taxis and tells them to wait. Then he follows with bags.

33.   RECEPTION HALL ROLAND'S HOUSE. It is perfectly bare. Briggs is just coming down the stairs carrying the one chair that is left, he puts it down, looks around at the bare hall, shakes his head sadly, dusts off the one chair, then looks up quickly at hearing bell ring, goes over to the door.

34.   FRONT OF ROLAND'S HOUSE. Briggs opens the door and lets Roland and Lord Howe-Greene in followed by Tom with bags.

35.   HALLWAY ROLAND'S HOUSE. Roland and Lord Howe-Greene enter, followed by Tom and Briggs. Briggs is delighted to see the old Englishman but is terribly chagrined at the condition of the house. He takes Lord Howe-Greene's coat and hat, and Roland engages Lord Howe-Greene in talking, then motions to Tom to get the chair into the library. Tom sneaks the chair around behind Lord Howe-Greene and into the library.

36.   LIBRARY. Tom sneaks the chair in, puts it down near the fireplace.

37.   HALLWAY ROLAND'S HOUSE. Roland noticing that Tom has the chair placed, escorts Lord Howe-Greene into the library with a grand flourish.

38.   LIBRARY. Tom is standing behind the chair. Lord Howe-Greene and Roland enter. Tom seats Lord Howe-Greene very ceremoniously in the chair. Lord Howe-Greene looks around the empty room and is astounded. He turns to Roland and says: *"I say, old fellow, the place looks rather beastly bare? Where's the furniture?"*
Roland thinks for a moment, looks at Tom; Tom does some quick heavy thinking and finally says, very graciously:

SP: "WE SENT THE FURNITURE OUT TO BE CLEANED IN HONOR OF YOUR COMING."
Roland smiles in relief and in approval of Tom, and then says:

SP: "THE CLEANERS ARE ON STRIKE SO THEY DIDN'T GET IT DONE IN TIME."
Lord Howe-Greene blandly accepts the explanation and thanks him for his thoughtfulness. Roland, who has been fondling the portfolio, can hardly wait for it to be opened, and he gives it to Lord Howe-Greene and then goes and stands by the mantel with Tom. Lord Howe-Greene fishes out the papers, finally comes to the will and starts to read the glad news. He reads for a moment and then

INSERT—"That providing said Roland Stone has carried out previous instructions of the will, his father provides as follows:"

Roland, overcome with impatience, begins to get even more interested. Lord Howe-Greene clears his throat and goes on reading:

INSERT—"I bequeath to my son, Roland Stone, one unencumbered position in the Anglo-American Insurance Co. as soliciting agent with a guarantee of $25.00 per week."

Roland looks in astonishment at Lord Howe-Greene as does also Tom. Lord Howe-Greene clears his throat again and goes on reading:

INSERT—"If at the end of one year, the business said Roland Stone procures for the company has proven profitable, the same will be a proof of his good business judgment, and he is then to come into possession of my entire fortune."

Roland stares simply open-mouthed in astonishment and disappointment, while Tom can hardly believe his ears.

INSERT—"If on the other hand, the company at the end of one year has suffered a loss through the agency of said Roland Stone, my entire fortune shall be given to the support of the Washington Home for Incurables."

Roland, absolutely dumbfounded by the news, stares at Lord Howe-Greene, then looks around at Tom. Tom looks at Roland accusingly.

Roland then turns in discouragement and asks Lord Howe-Greene if there's any more. Lord Howe-Greene goes on reading:

INSERT—"It is further provided that conditions under

which said Roland Stone is to work, shall be subject to the approval of Lord Howe-Greene." Roland is utterly unable to take all of this in, and he insists on reading it himself. Lord Howe-Greene hands it to him, and Roland starts in to read it as though he could hardly believe his eyes. Tom looks over his shoulder, and, finally disgusted with the whole proceeding, he goes over toward the window, stands there dejectedly and looks out.

39. STREET IN FRONT OF ROLAND'S HOUSE. Flash of the two taxis waiting, taken from an angle of the house.

40. LIBRARY ROLAND'S HOUSE. Tom receives a terrible shock on seeing the taxis and realizing that they can't pay them. He then goes over to Roland, and tells him that the two taxis are out there, eating their heads off. Roland looks out toward the window, thinks about the taxis, then looks over to Lord Howe-Greene, who is sitting comfortably in the last chair, thinks a moment, then goes over to Lord Howe-Greene, excuses himself, takes the chair from under the utterly flabbergasted Lord Howe-Greene, gives it to Tom and tells him to take it out to pay the taxis. Tom takes the chair and goes out, Lord Howe-Greene looking after him in wide-eyed astonishment. Roland then turns to Lord Howe-Greene and starts in to protest about the conditions of the will, but Lord Howe-Greene tells him that there is nothing that he can do. He takes the papers from Roland. Sits on window sill (especially built) and starts in to read the long document to Roland. Roland trying to follow Howe-Greene gets disgusted, leans against wall and at length slips to floor and sits there disconsolate, thinking of his rotten luck and of the girl away off with his rival. (Dissolve out.)

41. STUDIO GARDEN IN BUNKONIA. (Dissolve in.) Rosalie sitting in a hammock with Conwell standing near her, natives playing ukuleles, fanning them and giving them ice drinks, and Conwell whispering sweet nothings in Rosalie's ear. (Dissolve out.)

42.   LIBRARY ROLAND'S HOUSE. (Dissolve in.) Roland, sitting in the corner, very much distressed by the vision he has just seen. Lord Howe-Greene is still sitting on window sill reading document. Roland gives him a dirty look, puts his hands on his ears and at length jumps up and stalks out into the hall, leaving Howe-Greene still reading.

43.   HALLWAY—ROLAND'S HOUSE. Roland rushes in from library, looks back disgusted at Howe-Greene, who is still reading. At this moment Tom enters from street, goes to Roland, looks at him despondently, and says: *"What are we going to do now?"* Roland puts his hand on Tom's shoulder, and says with great emphasis:

SP: "LOOK HERE, TOM, YOU'VE GOT TO THINK OF SOME WAY TO GET ME TO ROSALIE!"

Tom thinks a moment, finally his face brightens and he says:

SP: "IF YOU'VE GOT TO SELL INSURANCE, WHY NOT SELL IT IN BUNKONIA?"

Roland is delighted at this, and tells Tom he knew he'd think up a way out—that they can start for Bunkonia to-morrow just as they had planned. Tom says of course they can. Roland says they will put it up to Lord Howe-Greene at once and they go into the library.

44.   LIBRARY, ROLAND'S HOUSE. Lord Howe-Greene still sitting reading. Roland and Tom enter, see him, and stop, both disgusted. Howe-Greene finishes his reading. Gets up and goes to them—gives Roland the document, tells him it is very important for him to keep it safe. Roland puts it in his pocket then turns to Howe-Greene and says:

SP: "I'VE BEEN THINKING THINGS OVER, AND I'VE DECIDED THAT IF I HAVE TO SELL INSURANCE, I WOULD LIKE VERY MUCH TO GET AWAY FROM WASHINGTON."

Lord Howe-Greene indicates that he understands his feelings in the matter, thinks a moment and says:

SP: "I HAVE IT! YOU SHALL TRY NEW YORK."

Roland looks at him in utter astonishment and says he is surprised that Lord Howe-Greene would suggest such a terrible place to sell insurance. He then turns to Tom and Tom agrees with him. Roland then says to Lord Howe-Greene,

SP: "NEW YORK WOULD NEVER DO! IT'S A TERRIBLE PLACE FOR INSURANCE!"

Lord Howe-Greene is interested, and wants to know why, and Roland goes on saying:

SP: "WHY THOUSANDS OF PEOPLE ARE KILLED THERE DAILY!"

Lord Howe-Greene is tremendously interested and surprised and wants to know how. Roland then goes on to describe the terrible life that New Yorkers lead and we fade out.

INSERT—Animated Cartoon of subway entrance—people pushing their way madly into the subway.

Interior of subway car. Animated Cartoon. Conductor is packing people in, smashing them in so they can hardly breathe and mashing them against the wall so that they collapse. He hammers others on the head with mallets to get them to move back. Everybody about him is mashed flat but still he pushes more in. (Fade out.)

Roland concludes his story about the terrible life in New York and Lord Howe-Greene greatly surprised at this says:

SP: "MY WORD!"

Roland appeals to Tom for confirmation and Tom nods his head and says that he hasn't heard the half of it. Lord Howe-Greene shakes his head, thinks a moment and says:

SP: "THEN YOU SHALL TRY CHICAGO!"

Roland is surprised at his suggesting Chicago, shakes his head, and says:

SP: "CHICAGO IS WORSE. PEOPLE ARE BLOWN TO DEATH IN CHICAGO BY MILLIONS!"

He turns to Tom and Tom confirms this and Lord Howe-Greene, extremely puzzled and surprised, wants to know how. Roland then goes

on to describe a scene of how people are blown to
death in Chicago, along Michigan Avenue. (Fade
out.)

INSERT—Animated Cartoon. (Fade in.) Michigan
Avenue. People are being blown down the Avenue and slammed up against walls where they
mash out flat. Some of them are blown over and
over and some of them are rolling like barrels.
(Fade out.)

Roland finishes his tale about Chicago, and Tom
agrees with him, shaking his head and saying:
"It is indeed a terrible sight to see this thing
that Roland just described!" Lord Howe-Greene
shows great distress, and shakes his head again
and exclaims:

SP: "MY WORD!"

Roland looks over at Tom and gives him a
wink. Tom gives Roland the high sign and the
two of them feel that things are going fine when
suddenly Lord Howe-Greene scratches his head
and gets a brilliant idea. He then tells Roland
that he has just the place for him and says:

SP: "I HAVE A COUSIN—A REAL ESTATE
AGENT IN LOS ANGELES—WHO WRITES
ME THAT THE CLIMATE IS SO SALUBRI-
OUS THAT EVERY ONE LIVES TO A RIPE
OLD AGE."

Roland looks at Lord Howe-Greene in astonishment, feeling that he has been stuck at last.
Lord Howe-Greene then pats him on the shoulder and says:

SP: "THAT'S THE PLACE FOR YOU, MY BOY!"

Roland looks genuinely alarmed and turns to
Tom for aid, but Tom himself is pretty much
stumped at this. Lord Howe-Greene feeling
that their problem has been settled, says that
that's exactly the place and everything will be
fine. Roland stalls, does some quick, heavy thinking, finally gets an idea, and says: "Lord Howe-
Greene, that's exactly where you're wrong."

SP: "THE TROUBLE OUT THERE IS THAT
PEOPLE NEVER DIE. THEY WON'T BUY
INSURANCE!"

Roland is rather pleased with himself for

thinking up this and Tom congratulates him on it, smiling his approbation. Lord Howe-Greene can hardly believe this angle of the situation, says he doesn't think that's possible. Roland, realizing that he has got to spike this says:

SP: "WHY, I TRIED TO SELL INSURANCE OUT THERE ONCE AND WHAT DO YOU THINK HAPPENED?"

Lord Howe-Greene is interested and wants to know what did happen to him. Tom looks rather quizzically at Roland, feeling that he is getting out beyond his depth. Roland clears his throat and starts in to describe what happened. (Fade out.)

45.   FRONT OF BUNGALOW IN LOS ANGELES. (Fade in.)

Three men with white whiskers to their waist are playing leap-frog on the lawn. Roland comes down the street, approaches one with an insurance circular in his hand and asks if he could interest him in some insurance. The old fellow says:

SP: "NO, I DON'T WANT ANY INSURANCE, BUT YOU MIGHT SEE PA."

Roland is surprised that a man of his age should have a father and asks where he is. The old fellow points to the front door of the bungalow and says:

SP: "HE'S HELPING GRANDPA CARRY THE PIANO UP IN GRANDMA'S ROOM."

Roland can hardly believe his ears at this and says: "What?" The old man nods and says:

SP: "YES, GRANDMA IS GOING TO TAKE MUSIC LESSONS."

Roland looks aghast at the old man who goes back to his leap-frog, and finally coming to, goes up to the house and rings the bell while the three old boys continue their leap-frog. Presently a youthful looking Jap with long, white whiskers opens the door. Roland asks for the father and is shown in.

46.   HALLWAY LOS ANGELES BUNGALOW. Roland enters with the Jap servant. Pa and

Grandpa—one with whiskers to the knees and one with whiskers to the ankles—are lifting a piano up the stairs. Roland approaches pa and asks him if he could interest him in insurance. Pa holds the piano with one hand, with the other takes the young man's circular and looks at it. He then shakes his head no, turns to grandpa and says: "Father, do you want any insurance?" Grandpa asks to see the circular and Pa hands it up to him. Grandpa looks at it a minute, then looks at Roland, shakes his head and says:

SP: "I THINK NOT, SON. I CAN LOOK AFTER MY FAMILY FOR A FEW YEARS YET, AND BY THAT TIME THEY'LL BE ABLE TO TAKE CARE OF THEMSELVES."

He hands the circular back to Roland and he and Pa pick up the piano and go on upstairs, Roland looking after them in absolute amazement. (Fade out.)

47. LIBRARY, ROLAND'S HOUSE. (Fade in.) Roland finishes his story about Los Angeles. Turns to Tom who confirms everything he has said. Lord Howe-Greene, shaking his head in amazement over these extraordinary conditions in America, says very weakly—

SP: "MY WORD" (in very small type).

And Lord Howe-Greene is very much distressed. He feels that this case is baffling him. He finally looks up hopelessly and asks Roland what they're going to do. Roland, puzzled, turns to Tom and asks him what he thinks of the situation. Tom thinks a moment, finally gets an idea, turns to Lord Howe-Greene and says:

SP: "IF YOU COULD ONLY GET HIM TO GO DOWN TO BUNKONIA."

Roland pooh-poohs this idea and says no, he never would, he couldn't go there because it is too far away. But Tom goes on into raptures about Bunkonia, telling him what a marvelous place it is for business of all kinds, and Lord Howe-Greene, glad of some solution to his problem, finally jumps at the idea— turns to Roland and says:

SP: "THAT'S AN IDEA! NEW COUNTRY—
VIRGIN FIELD—IT'S JUST THE PLACE
FOR YOU!"
Roland thinks a minute as though he had to
be convinced, but Lord Howe-Greene keeps on
begging him to take a chance. Tom joins Lord
Howe-Greene in urging him, and finally Roland
allows himself to be persuaded, decides that he
will go, Lord Howe-Greene shakes him warmly
by the hand and—(fade out).

T: SANTO GRAFTO, CAPITOL OF BUNK-
ONIA, THE BEAUTIFUL LAND OF SUN-
SHINE AND FLOWERS, MUSIC AND
LAUGHTER, TAMALES, TYPHOID AND
PTOMAINE.

48.   EXTERIOR VIEW OF TOWN OF SANTO
GRAFTO. (Fade in.) Showing natives, equi-
pages, a few soldiers, etc. (Dissolve out.)

49.   PARK (dissolve in) SINGERS, DANCERS,
MUSICIANS, FLOWER SELLERS, CHIL-
DREN, ETC. (Dissolve out.)

T: KING CARAMBA AND HIS COUNCIL EN-
GAGED IN THEIR FAVORITE INDOOR
SPORT OF RAISING TAXES AND DOWN-
ING LIQUOR.

50.   THE KING'S COUNCIL CHAMBER. Caramba
sitting at the head of the table with three councilors on his right and three on his left—among
them being Enrico. Some servants in livery are
standing about. One of the councilors has just
finished reading the text of a bill to raise the
taxes. King Caramba is sound asleep with a
bottle in his hand. Enrico, the only sober one
in the lot, is looking in a sinister, calculating way
around the table. The councilor who is reading
the bill sways as he reads and the paper jiggles
in his hand.

51.   INSERT PAPER RAISING TAXES. The
councilor finishes reading, puts paper in front of
King and guides his hand while he signs it.

INSERT—King's hand is signing the paper—it wanders
all over the paper so that most of the name is
written on the table with a grand flourish at the
end.

After signing the paper, the king takes another drink. The man takes the paper and blows on it. Enrico, with a sinister smile, gets up and starts to go. The Councilor takes the paper, waves it aloft to the other councilors who cheer in a drunken manner. They all pour out another bumper, Enrico stands by the doorway in a calculating manner, then smiling a satisfied smile, he turns on his heel and leaves. (Fade out.)

T: THE REVOLUTIONISTS AWAIT THEIR LEADER AT THEIR RENDEZVOUS IN THE RUE DE STILETTO.

52. REVOLUTIONISTS' RENDEZVOUS. (Fade in.) A number of revolutionary leaders are there, including the Countess, Conwell, the General and two men in citizen's clothes. They are discussing matters more or less violently and waiting for Enrico.

53. RENDEZVOUS AT GATE. Enrico enters, looks about stealthily, sees that no one is watching and then wraps three times on the gate. The gate is opened by a villainous servant and Enrico enters.

54. REVOLUTIONISTS' RENDEZVOUS. The revolutionists are still talking together and they see Enrico entering. They gather about him to get the news and Enrico says:

SP: "THEY WERE *ALL* DRUNK TO-NIGHT. IT WILL SOON BE TIME TO STRIKE."

They all rejoice at this. Enrico asks the General about the army and he replies:

SP: "TWO HUNDRED OF THE ARMY ARE WITH US NOW. IT WILL TAKE A HUNDRED PESETAS TO WIN OVER THE OTHER FIFTY."

Enrico is very angry at this, and asks him what he means by a hundred pesetas, and is very sore at the tremendous cost at buying these men. The Countess stops his raving, putting her finger over his lips, goes into her stocking, takes out the money and gives the General two bills, which amount to more than he has asked for. He then turns to Conwell and starts in to talk. The

General puts the money in his pocket but Enrico notices him and says:

SP: "HERE! HERE! GIVE US THE CHANGE!"

Reluctantly the General digs it up, starts to pass it over to the Countess but Enrico stops him before the Countess notices, grabs the money and puts it in his own pocket. Enrico then crosses over to Conwell and says:

SP: "ARE YOU SURE WE CAN HANDLE OLD BIRD WHEN WE'RE READY?"

Conwell tells him it's the easiest thing in the world, that the old man has got to do just what he says and winds up with:

SP: "DIDN'T I GET HIM THIS JOB?"

They all seem satisfied with this and go on plotting. (Fade out.)

T: ON THE EDGE OF THIS POLITICAL VOL-CANO SITS OUR OLD FRIEND, COLONEL BIRD, AT PEACE WITH ALL THE WORLD IN THE FULLNESS OF HIS IGNORANCE.

55.   COLONEL BIRD'S ROOM IN THE CONSU-LATE. (Dissolve in.) Colonel Bird is sitting at his desk reading a political book. Mammy is straightening room and dusting. Rosalie enters dressed for the street. She goes to the Colonel, looks over his shoulder, tells him that he works too hard, makes him promise he will get some rest and kisses him good-by and goes out.

56.   CONWELL'S ROOM IN THE CONSULATE. Conwell is sitting at his desk very busily but rather slyly making out a report. Rosalie comes from her father's room, says good morning to Conwell and starts to pass through. Conwell immediately jumps to his feet, comes to her, and stops her, admiring her dress, etc. Rosalie shows by her attitude that she has begun to fear this man. She starts to pass him but he takes her by the hand, restrains her and says:

SP: "HOW MUCH LONGER ARE YOU GOING TO KEEP ME WAITING?"

Rosalie is embarrassed and doesn't know what to say. She tells him that she doesn't care about him in that way and he finally says:

SP: "DON'T YOU THINK YOU OWE ME SOME-

THING AFTER ALL I'VE DONE FOR YOUR FATHER?"

She expresses her gratitude for the help he has been to her father but doesn't quite see why she should marry him for that reason. Conwell is getting impatient and finally says:

SP: "YOUR FATHER AS GOOD AS PROMISED THAT YOU'D MARRY ME."

Rosalie is surprised and incredulous, says she doesn't believe it and turns and goes to the door. Conwell tries to restrain her but doesn't succeed. Rosalie calls in to her father and asks if he will come in.

57.   COLONEL BIRD'S ROOM AT CONSULATE. Colonel Bird puts down his book and goes in to Conwell's room.

58.   CONWELL'S ROOM AT CONSULATE. Rosalie looks up at her father almost in tears and asks if he promised that she marry Conwell. Colonel Bird berates Conwell for suggesting such a thing, tells her she shall marry the man of her choice. Conwell protests that Bird is indebted to him for his job, Colonel Bird straightens himself up with great dignity and says:

SP: "WELL, SIR, DIDN'T I MAKE YOU MY SECRETARY?"

Conwell looks at him as much as to say— "You poor old simp—just wait." Colonel Bird takes Rosalie to the door, kisses her good-by and she goes out. He then turns to Conwell and tells him to stop annoying his daughter.

59.   EXTERIOR CONSULATE. Rosalie comes out and goes down the street toward the station.

60.   CONWELL'S ROOM AT CONSULATE. Colonel Bird is still laying down the law to Conwell who nods his head, and Colonel Bird goes back to his own room. Conwell looks after him in a menacing way, then shakes his fist after him and suggesting that he will get even with him yet. He then gets his hat and goes out. (Fade out.)

T:
61.   RAILWAY STATION AT SANTO GRAFTO. Station master is there, baggage man, three or

four natives, some kids and several pretty native girls. Rosalie also is waiting. The train comes in, a couple of soldiers get off and greet the girls. Two natives get off and then Tom and Roland get off. Rosalie rushes to them. Roland kisses her, she greets Tom and leads them off.

62. BACK OF SANTO GRAFTO STATION. Carriage waiting with native driver. Rosalie enters with Roland and Tom, they get into the carriage and drive off. (Fade out.)

T: THE HOTEL DEL MOSQUITO.

63. FRONT OF HOTEL. (Fade in.) There are several tables in front of the hotel and also several booths and a sign over the entrance. Several people are sitting at the tables drinking. At one table sits the Countess and Enrico. Conwell enters and joins them, rather sore over his rebuff by Rosalie. They ask him why so grouchy and he tells them. They give him the laugh but Enrico slaps him on the back and tells him she will come around all right. Waiters are going in and out. A pretty girl is selling flowers, a couple of musicians are playing guitars. Carriage drives up with Rosalie, Roland and Tom. Tom and Roland get out, a native porter comes from the hotel and takes their bags into the hotel followed by Tom, while Roland stops to speak to Rosalie. Conwell looks up, sees Roland and is very much disturbed. He calls the attention of his two friends to Roland and tells them who he is and they all look searchingly at him. Roland says a very affectionate good-by to Rosalie and says:

SP: "MAY I COME TO SEE YOU THIS EVENING?"

Rosalie tells him that he may, bids him good-by and he watches her drive away, sighs and turns and goes into hotel. Conwell half hides so that Roland won't see him. After he is well out of sight Conwell starts to grumble at his ill luck at having this fellow come down here. Enrico pats him on the back, whispers in his ear and says:

SP: "WE CAN PUT HIM OUT OF THE WAY DURING THE REVOLUTION."

The Countess nods that this will be easy but Conwell looks doubtful, shakes his head and says:

SP: "NO, IT WOULD BE DANGEROUS FOR US—HE'S TOO WELL KNOWN IN WASHINGTON."

Conwell shows his anger and chagrin at the turn of affairs. Enrico shrugs his shoulders but the Countess starts in to think of some way out.

64. HALLWAY OUTSIDE ROLAND'S APARTMENT. Porter enters with Roland and Tom, opens door and they enter Roland's room.

65. ROLAND'S APARTMENT IN THE HOTEL. The porter shows Tom and Roland in. Roland is quite pleased with the place, tips the porter generously; the porter leaves, followed by Tom and his bag.

66. FRONT OF HOTEL. Conwell is still cursing his luck. Enrico is sympathetic but helpless. The Countess is thinking heavily and finally gets an idea. She leans over, pats Conwell on the hand and says:

SP: "THERE'S SOMETHING ON EVERY MAN IF YOU CAN ONLY FIND IT. LEAVE IT TO ME. I'LL FIND SOMETHING TO HANG ON HIM."

Enrico approves of this, Conwell is slightly interested and the Countess goes on explaining that she has tackled many a difficult proposition and won out. Just to leave it to her. (Fade out.)

T: EVENING.

67. BEAUTIFUL COURTYARD OR GARDEN AT THE CONSULATE.

Roland, dinner coat, and Rosalie, evening dress, and the Colonel are there. Roland has just finished telling the story of his dad's directions regarding his fortune and he finishes up by saying to Rosalie:

SP: "SO WE'VE GOT TO WAIT ANOTHER YEAR, ROSALIE."

She takes his hand and says she doesn't mind at all, she knows he'll be a great success. The old Colonel comes to him, takes him by the hand and says:

SP: "I'M GLAD SOMETHING HAS SET YOU TO WORK, BUT YOU'VE GOT TO WIN TO GET ROSALIE."

Roland thanks the Colonel, tells him he knows it and that he's going to make good. The Colonel rather brusquely tells him he hopes he does and then leaves. Rosalie runs to Roland, tells him she knows he's going to make good.

68. HALLWAY OUTSIDE ROLAND'S APARTMENT. The Countess enters, looks around stealthily, goes to the door, tries it, finds it locked, takes a hairpin from her hair, unlocks the door with it, looks around and enters.

69. ROLAND'S ROOM IN HOTEL. The Countess in dark evening dress enters and closes the door. Begins to rummage around among Roland's things in his wardrobe trunk. She finally uncovers a lot of blank insurance policies. She shows great interest in the discovery of the papers, as papers are one of her main stock in trade. She starts feverishly to examine them.

INSERT—HANDFUL OF INSURANCE BLANKS.

The Countess looks at them in disgust, puts them back where she found them and goes on hunting.

70. GARDEN OF CONSULATE. Another very beautiful shot with Rosalie and Roland standing or sitting on a bench planning their future.

71. ROLAND'S BEDROOM IN HOTEL. The Countess still rummaging around. Down in the bottom drawer of the trunk, she discovers a copy of Roland's father's instructions which have been given him by Lord Howe-Greene. She pounces on this and reads it.

INSERT—If at the end of one year the business said Roland Stone procures for the company has proven profitable, the same will be proof of his good business judgment and he is then to come into possession of my entire fortune.

Countess ponders over this a moment, then reads next paragraph:

INSERT—Part of statement as follows:

"If, on the other hand, the company at the end of one year has suffered a loss through the agency of said Roland Stone, my entire fortune shall be given to the support of the Washington Home for Incurables."

The Countess gloats over this discovery, carefully replaces everything just as she found it, conceals the paper in her dress and stealthily leaves the room.

72. EXTERIOR OF CONSULATE. Roland is just bidding Rosalie good-night. She is expressing her good wishes for his success. Roland looks out toward the view of Bunkonia, then turns to Rosalie and says:

SP: "WHY, IN A VIRGIN FIELD LIKE THIS, I CAN'T HELP BUT MAKE THE COMPANY MONEY."

Rosalie is just as certain as he is about it. He then goes on telling her that in just one little year he will be claiming her. Rosalie is delighted. Roland timidly kisses her, says good-night and leaves. Rosalie looks after him and sighs.

73. CAFE OF THE HOTEL. Enrico and Conwell sitting at a table smoking and drinking. Conwell is quite nervous and irritable. Enrico is trying to jolly him up. The Countess enters in a very mysterious way, sits beside them and tells them with much glee but in great secretiveness that she has great news. She stealthily draws the paper from her dress and shows it to them.

INSERT—SAME CLAUSE AS BEFORE WITH THE COUNTESS' FINGER POINTING TO IT.

Conwell and Enrico are puzzled over this, and Conwell asks the Countess how it concerns him. The Countess looks furtively about and says:

SP: "DON'T YOU SEE—IF HE LOSES MONEY FOR THE COMPANY, HE LOSES THE FORTUNE AND THE GIRL!"

Enrico and Conwell consider this for a moment, and finally realize the truth of it but ask the Countess what she has in her bean. The Countess looks furtively about and says:

SP: "WE'LL HAVE HIM INSURE THE LIVES OF THE KING AND COUNCIL."

Enrico and Conwell look at her, then at each

other and ask what good that will do. The
,   Countess looks at them in a surprised way and
says:
SP: "AREN'T THEY ALL TO BE KILLED IN
OUR REVOLUTION?"
Slowly the force of this breaks over the minds
of Enrico and Conwell, their faces become
wreathed in smiles, at length both laugh boister-
ously. Conwell takes the paper and looks at it
again, then rises, takes his glass, holds it out
toward the Countess and says:
SP: "TO THE WOMEN—BLESS THEM. WHAT
WOULD WE DO WITHOUT THEM?"
He and Enrico raise their glasses and drink
to the Countess who smiles and blushes. (Fade
out.)
T: THE NEXT MORNING—THE PLANT.
74.   FRONT OF THE HOTEL. (Fade in.) Roland
is sitting at a table in the f.g. having his breakfast. Conwell and Enrico come to the hotel
doorway and look out. They finally spot Roland.
Conwell then gives instructions to Enrico as to
what to do. He then goes out toward Roland
while Enrico backs into the hotel doorway and
waits. Conwell goes over to Roland, slaps him
on the back, greets him heartily. Roland rises,
rather embarrassed, Conwell shakes his hand
cordially and sits beside him. Enrico in the
doorway watches with a sinister smile. Conwell
asks Roland what he is doing down in Bunkonia.
Roland says:
SP: "I'VE COME DOWN TO SELL INSUR-
ANCE."
Conwell is interested in this and Roland tells
him in a few words what he wants to do. Conwell is quite interested and says:
SP: "PERHAPS I CAN GIVE YOU A BOOST. I
KNOW ALL THE BIG GUNS DOWN
HERE."
Roland is mildly interested but not overly
enthusiastic as he knows something of Conwell's
boasting proclivities. However he thanks him.
Conwell offers Roland a cigarette and while Ro-

land is taking it, Conwell quickly signals to
Enrico. Enrico sees the signal and walks down
to the front of the hotel. Conwell looks up
sharply, pretending he has just seen Enrico,
points him out to Roland, who looks also, and
Conwell then speaks, saying:

SP: "THAT'S ENRICO DE CASTANET, SECRE-
TARY OF WAR, AND A GREAT PAL OF
KING CARAMBA."
Roland is quite impressed. Conwell says he
will bring him over and gets up and goes over
toward Enrico. Enrico turns, sees him, greets
him very enthusiastically, saying, "Ah, my
friend," shakes his hand and raises his hat at
the same time Conwell is doing it. Conwell
then asks him if he won't come over and meet
his friend, at the same time giving Enrico the
wink. Enrico says he will be pleased and they
both go over to Roland's table. Conwell introduces Enrico to Roland. Enrico again
raises his hat. They all sit, Roland orders
drinks and Conwell briefly tells Enrico about
Roland's business. Enrico says he is interested in any friend of Conwell's and after a
few words of explanation from Roland, Enrico
says to Conwell:

SP: "THERE'S A MEETING OF THE COUNCIL
TO-NIGHT. WHY NOT BRING YOUR
FRIEND? I'LL HAVE HIM MEET THE
KING."
Roland is quite overcome by all this kindness,
and Conwell says: *"That is exactly the thing to
do."* Conwell takes his drink, holds it up and
says:

SP: "HERE'S HOPING YOU INSURE THE
LIVES OF THE KING AND ALL HIS
COUNCIL."
They all drink to Roland's success. Roland is
overcome by their kindness. (Fade out.)

T: AT THE COUNCIL MEETING.
75.   KING CARAMBA'S COUNCIL ROOM. (Fade
in.) King Caramba and his councilors are there,
boozing as usual. Conwell is standing making a

speech to them which they are not listening to very intently. Conwell is telling them what a great thing insurance is, and says:

SP: "RIGHT AT YOUR VERY DOOR, GENTLE-MEN, IS A YOUNG YANKEE WHO IS ABLE TO SELL YOU THIS WONDERFUL LIFE INSURANCE."

The councilors listen in a drunken way, all except old Señor Frijole, who is very sore and grouchy and signifies that he wants nothing to do with this Yankee and his business. Enrico rises to speak, telling them what a wonderful thing insurance is, and then he says:

SP: "WHY, DO YOU REALIZE, GENTLEMEN, THAT WE GET THOUSANDS OF PESETAS FOR A MERE FEW HUNDRED?"

He turns to Conwell and asks him if he is right. Conwell assures him he is right, and then continues his speech. At this the Councilors begin to take very much more interest. They signify that this must be very good after all, all except old Señor Frijole, who is sitting next to Enrico. He pulls Enrico's sleeve and says:

SP: "BUT YOU HAVE TO DIE TO GET IT—DON'T YOU?"

Enrico gives him a quick, dirty look, tells him to shut up, which squelches him somewhat, but he goes on mumbling to himself. Conwell goes on talking, saying that this opportunity should not be overlooked. He sits down. Enrico says he thinks it is a fine idea and says:

SP: "I'LL TAKE 10,000 PESETAS MYSELF."

At this the councilors are more interested than ever as they know Enrico is not the type to be done. Old Frijole goes on grumbling into his glass of liquor saying he will have nothing to do with it. Conwell goes over to the door, opens it and goes out.

76. HALLWAY IN PALACE. Roland sitting on a settee. Conwell comes from Council Room. Roland with application in his hand jumps up nervously and meets him. Conwell tells him it is all right and they go into Council Room.

77. COUNCIL ROOM. Conwell brings Roland in

and introduces him to the councilors who greet
him with drunken enthusiasm, while Conwell
stands in the background with a menacing leer.
Roland is very much pleased, but bashful, overcome by his luck. Enrico, with a grand flourish,
asks Roland for an application which Roland
gives him, and he signs his own application with
a grand flourish and hands it over to Roland
as if to say—"There, what more assurance do
you want that this is a good thing?" At this
the other councilors all reach out drunkenly and
grab applications, Roland writing in the amounts,
and all of them signing the applications drunkenly. Enrico and Conwell exchange triumphant
looks, but old Señor Frijole shows his disgust
for the entire affair. He finally goes up and
tries to keep the King from signing his application, but the King gives him a push, he staggers
back into his chair, mumbling and grumbling
and warning them against Yankee tricks. By this
time, Roland has most of the applications signed,
Conwell comes up, pats him on the back and
congratulates him. (Fade out.)

T: ABOUT A WEEK LATER. (Fade in.)
78.   COLONEL BIRD'S ROOM IN CONSULATE.
Rosalie in simple evening dress is standing by
the window. Roland, in a blue coat and flannel
trousers, rushes in and Rosalie runs to him. He
tells her he has a surprise for her. She is very
much interested and wants to know what it is.
He says:

SP: "I'VE INSURED KING CARAMBA AND HIS
COUNCILORS FOR NEARLY A HUNDRED
THOUSAND DOLLARS."
Rosalie is amazed and delighted at this good
news. Roland says:

SP: "I JUST DELIVERED THE POLICIES AND
COLLECTED THE PREMIUMS."
Rosalie is in ecstasies and throws her arm
around him and kisses him, much to his embar-
rassment, although he is also greatly pleased.
Roland says:

SP: "I WANT YOU TO COME OUT TO HELP
CELEBRATE MY GOOD FORTUNE."

She is delighted, picks up a tulle scarf and goes out with Roland.

79. CONWELL'S ROOM IN CONSULATE. Conwell is standing at desk as Roland and Rosalie enter. Conwell turns to them smiling. Roland stops and tells Rosalie Conwell's influence got him his big clients. He goes to Conwell and thanks him, shaking his hand. Rosalie is surprised and puzzled that Conwell should help Roland. Roland gets Rosalie and they go out bidding Conwell good-night. Conwell looks after them leering.

80. EXTERIOR CONSULATE. Roland and Rosalie come out of the Consulate and leave in the direction of the hotel.

81. REVOLUTIONISTS' RENDEZVOUS. The Countess, three other Revolutionists and about thirty soldiers are there. They are all excited and talking among themselves.

82. GATEWAY OF RENDEZVOUS. General enters hurriedly and knocks three times—gate opens and he quickly enters.

83. REVOLUTIONISTS' RENDEZVOUS. Revolutionists talking and awaiting somebody. The general enters and joins group. He looks about and says:

SP: "ENRICO HAS JUST LEFT THE COUNCIL MEETING. AS SOON AS HE COMES WE STRIKE."

He then leaves and goes to soldiers—the others discuss this news excitedly.

84. GATEWAY OF RENDEZVOUS. A group of six or eight soldiers, led by a sergeant, approach skulkingly—the sergeant knocks at the gate, which opens and the soldiers all sneak in.

85. EXTERIOR CONSULATE. Colonel enters from opposite direction taken by Roland and Rosalie and enters consulate. Four guards look out from hiding places.

86. CAFE IN FRONT OF THE HOTEL (NIGHT). Several people at tables. Roland and Rosalie enter and go into one of the little booths and sit down—waiter comes and takes their order—they are very happy.

87. EXTERIOR CONSULATE. Enrico enters, whistles softly, and four guards sneak out of hiding places and come to him. He asks if Colonel Bird is home. They tell him he has just gone in. He tells them to wait in the shadow and they go into the shadow and Enrico, looking about cautiously, goes to the porch and knocks three times.

88. CONWELL'S ROOM IN CONSULATE. Conwell at desk hears knock, glances toward the colonel's room and goes to the door, opens it. Enrico quickly enters. Conwell closes the door. Enrico asks him if the Colonel is in. He smiles and says yes. Enrico tells him he has come to fix old Bird. Conwell says: "Easy—he'll do anything you say," and tells him to wait a moment and goes into the Colonel's room.

89. COLONEL'S ROOM. Colonel at his desk. Conwell enters, tells him that Enrico de Castanet wishes to see him. Colonel somewhat surprised and a little bit flattered, swells up a bit, tells Conwell to show Señor de Castanet in. Conwell opens the door and de Castanet enters. The Colonel greets him and they sit down and Conwell goes out and they begin to talk, Enrico telling him that they are going to pull a revolution that night and put King Caramba and his council out of the way.

90. CAFE IN FRONT OF HOTEL. Roland and Rosalie still dining, having a grand time. A couple of revolutionists enter and sit in the booth next to theirs.

91. COLONEL'S ROOM. Enrico is talking very earnestly to the Colonel. At length he says:

SP: "NOW IF YOU WILL ADVISE THE AMERICAN PRESIDENT TO RECOGNIZE OUR NEW GOVERNMENT TO-MORROW, IT WILL MEAN ALMOST ANYTHING YOU WISH TO ASK."

The old Colonel is puzzled and vaguely alarmed at this, doesn't quite get it. Asks Enrico:

SP: "ARE YOU OFFERING ME A BRIBE?"

Enrico shrugs his shoulders and says if that is what he chooses to call it. The old Colonel becomes very angry, rises at his desk, begins to lay down the law to Enrico and says:

SP: "YOU WOULD HAVE ME BARTER THE HONOR OF MY COUNTRY? ARE YOU AWARE, SIR, THAT YOU ARE DEALING WITH *A LOYAL AMERICAN CITIZEN?*"

He bangs the table, stretches himself to his full height. Enrico rises and tries to argue with him, but the Colonel brushes him away and grandiloquently points to American flag.

SP: "THAT, SIR, IS THE GREATEST FLAG IN THE WORLD, AND NO ACT OF MINE SHALL EVER STAIN IT."

At the finish of the speech, the old Colonel, with a grand flourish, orders Enrico out of the room. Enrico backs out, protesting all the way. The old man kicking him out at the finish.

92.   CONWELL'S OFFICE. Conwell waiting expectantly. Enrico lands in the room, to which he has been catapulted by the old Colonel's foot. Conwell comes to him, much perturbed.

93.   COL. BIRD'S ROOM AT THE CONSULATE. Old Colonel slams the door and walks up and down in excitement.

94.   CONWELL'S ROOM. Enrico angrily telling Conwell what happened in the other room. Conwell very sore and disgusted at the old man, says:

SP: "HAVE YOUR GUARD KIDNAP HIM AND LOCK HIM UP AND *I'LL* TAKE CHARGE OF THE CONSULATE."

Enrico angrily approves of this and rushes outdoors.

95.   COLONEL'S ROOM AT CONSULATE. Colonel at his desk, rapidly writing a telegram, presses button.

96.   CONWELL'S ROOM AT CONSULATE. Conwell, looking out, hears the button, goes into the Colonel's room.

97.   COLONEL'S ROOM AT CONSULATE. Colonel finishing telegram, rises. Conwell comes to him. Colonel indignantly tells him in a very few words what has happened, points to the flag, hammers his chest in great indignation, shows

him a telegram which he is sending. Conwell
reads telegram:

INSERT—TELEGRAM.

> TO CAPT. HENRY HALYARD, U. S. BAT-
> TLESHIP UTAH, PORTO PUNKO, BUNK-
> ONIA.
> REVOLUTION THREATENED HERE TO-
> NIGHT. SEND MARINES AT ONCE TO
> PROTECT AMERICAN INTERESTS.
>   BIRD,
>   CONSUL.

Conwell smiles at this. The Colonel orders him
to send it at once and Conwell, still smiling,
starts to leave the room, when the door opens
and in bursts Enrico with his four guards. He
tells them to arrest the Colonel, which they do,
but the old boy puts up a fight. They finally
overcome him and hold him prisoner. He appeals to Conwell, who only laughs at him and
tears up the telegram and throws it in his face,
shakes his finger at the old man and says:

SP: "WE SHALL SEE NOW WHO IS THE BOSS
      AROUND HERE."

The old Colonel is annoyed and tries to get
at Conwell but the guards hold him. Conwell
smiles and says:

SP: "WE SHALL SEE NOW WHETHER I GET
      YOUR DAUGHTER OR NOT."

He tells the guard to rush the old man out,
which they do, followed by Conwell and Enrico.

98.   CONWELL'S ROOM IN CONSULATE. The
      guards rush the old Colonel through the room
      and out, followed by Conwell and Enrico.

99.   FRONT OF THE CONSULATE. Guards rush
      the old Colonel out followed by Enrico and Con-
      well. Enrico tells the guard:

SP: "LOCK HIM UP IN THE DUNGEONS
      UNDER THE PALACE."

He scribbles on a card that he gives to one
of the guards. The guards rush the Colonel off
toward the palace and Enrico and Conwell go
in the opposite direction, toward the rendezvous.

100. CAFE IN FRONT OF HOTEL. (Long shot)
      showing the two booths, with Roland and Rosalie

in one and the two revolutionists in the other.
CLOSE UP OF TABLE WITH ROLAND AND RO-
SALIE. They are talking animatedly. Roland
has a little notebook in his hand, which he shows
to Rosalie and says:
SP: "THINK WHAT THIS MEANS TO US, RO-
SALIE! I CAN'T FAIL NOW."
Rosalie is delighted at the wonder of this—
takes his hand and they go on talking of their
plans.
CLOSE UP OF THE TABLE WITH THE REVOLU-
TIONISTS. A third revolutionist officer comes
in hurriedly, sits down, looks about and says:
SP: "THE HOUR TO STRIKE IS AT HAND."
The other revolutionists listen.
CLOSE UP OF ROLAND AND ROSALIE. They are
pricking up their ears.
CLOSE UP OF REVOLUTIONISTS' TABLE. One
asks the newcomer what is going to happen
and he says:
SP: "THE REVOLUTION STARTS TO-NIGHT."
The other two gloat over this.
CLOSE UP—Roland and Rosalie listen, their alarm
growing, Roland climbs on chair and looks into
next booth.
OTHER BOOTH—Roland looking over top, frightened.
The revolutionists go on talking, the newcomer
says:
SP: "KING CARAMBA AND HIS COUNCIL
WILL BE KILLED FIRST."
They go on talking together.
CLOSE UP, ROLAND AND ROSALIE—Roland is dis-
mayed at what he has heard. Rosalie starts to
speak and he tells her to keep quiet and he listens
over the partition.
CLOSE UP, THREE REVOLUTIONISTS—They are
talking, call waiter, pay him and get up and
leave hurriedly. Roland ducks down.
CLOSE UP OF ROLAND—Finally he realizes what is
to happen, and that it means ruin and he turns
to Rosalie and says:
SP: "THEY ARE GOING TO KILL EVERY ONE
I'VE INSURED."
They are both terribly alarmed and realize

that this means ruin for their hopes. They don't
know what to do, at length Rosalie says:

SP: "WE MUST HAVE FATHER SEND FOR
        HELP."

Roland in his terror agrees to this—he throws
a bill on the table, she grabs him by the hand and
they rush out.

101.   EXTERIOR REVOLUTIONISTS' RENDEZ-
        VOUS—Enrico and Conwell enter. Enrico
        knocks on door three times, the door is opened
        and they enter.

102.   REVOLUTIONISTS' RENDEZVOUS. Enrico
        and Conwell enter and join Countess and General
        and tell them the time has come to strike—that
        old Bird refused Enrico's request, that they
        chucked him in prison and Conwell now is boss
        of the Consulate.

103.   DUNGEONS UNDER PALACE. Four guards
        rush in Colonel Bird and chuck him in one of
        the cells, lock the door and rush out.

104.   EXTERIOR CONSULATE. Roland and Ro-
        salie run in and rush into the Consulate.

105.   CONWELL'S ROOM AT CONSULATE. Ro-
        land and Rosalie rush through.

106.   COL. BIRD'S ROOM AT CONSULATE. Ro-
        land and Rosalie rush in—see the overturned
        furniture and realize something has happened.
        Mammy enters from back door. Rosalie runs to
        her and asks what has happened and she doesn't
        know. Rosalie asks Mammy where her father is.
        Mammy says she left him here. Rosalie is terri-
        fied. Rosalie and the old servant rush out. Ro-
        salie upstairs and Mammy to kitchen to look for
        the Colonel. Roland picks up the bits of the
        telegram from the floor and pieces them together.

Rosalie comes back into the room and the old
servant enters and shakes her head. Rosalie in
terror, says:

SP: "FATHER IS NOT HERE."

Roland thinks a moment, realizes that they have
taken him away, shows his anger at this, calls
Rosalie to him, finishes piecing the telegram together and then reads it.

INSERT OF TELEGRAM PIECED TOGETHER.

Rosalie having read the telegram shows hope in her face and says to Roland:

SP: "YOU MUST SEND THAT MESSAGE AT ONCE."

Roland jumps at this and gathers up the pieces in his hand, starts to go, then thinks of the girl, stops and asks her what she will do in the meantime. She says never to mind, but to go on, old Mammy will stay with her. Roland is reluctant to go, but Rosalie goes to the drawer of the desk, takes out her father's old army revolver, and then goes to Roland and says:

SP: "I AM AN AMERICAN GIRL AND CAN TAKE CARE OF MYSELF."

She tells him to go and forces him out toward the door. He takes her in his arms and kisses her and rushes out. The old mammy comes to her and puts her arm about her.

107. FRONT OF CONSULATE—Roland rushes out and down the street toward the station.

108. REVOLUTIONISTS' RENDEZVOUS. The Countess, the General and a few other officers, about 100 soldiers and a major are there. Enrico is giving his instructions to the various people. Conwell and Enrico enter. Conwell tells Countess, General and others what has happened and tells them what to do. Conwell says:

SP: "LOOK HERE, WHAT ABOUT THE GIRL? I WANT HER ABDUCTED AND KEPT FOR ME IN THE PALACE."

Enrico says that's all right—tells the general to put a guard at the disposal of Conwell. Conwell and the general leave—go to soldiers. Enrico tells Countess to look after the girl when she gets to the palace. Countess says she will and Enrico goes on talking to others.

About 100 soldiers are there. Conwell and General enter. General selects a guard of about three men. Tells them to obey Conwell's orders and Conwell leaves with the three men. The General then turns to the rest of the soldiers instructing them as to what they are to do.

109. EXTERIOR R. R. STATION. Roland runs in and enters station.

110. INTERIOR R. R. STATION AND TELE-
GRAPH OFFICE. Roland rushes in and tells
station master he wants to send a message. Starts
to write it. Station master stops him—says he
cannot send message. Roland asks why. Station
master points to telegraph instrument.
CLOSE UP OF TELEGRAPH INSTRUMENT
SMASHED.
   Roland asks who did that. Station master says:
SP: "THE REVOLUTIONISTS."
   Roland is nonplused for the moment—rushes
out of the door, followed by the station master.

111. EXTERIOR R. R. STATION. Roland rushes
out followed by station master. Roland runs in
the direction of the hotel. Station master looks
after him and bites his thumb at him, then goes
back into station.

112. EXTERIOR WINDOW SIDE OF CONSU-
LATE. Conwell sneaks in with his three soldiers
and peeks in window and sees—

113. COL. BIRD'S ROOM IN CONSULATE—Rosalie sitting tense holding gun and watching
door. Mammy beside her standing.

114. EXTERIOR WINDOW SIDE OF CONSU-
LATE. Conwell shows his chagrin at the fact
of Rosalie's having a gun, thinks a moment, then
tells his guard to keep very quiet and follow
him. He sneaks out toward front of house, followed by guard very quietly.

115. CAFE IN FRONT OF HOTEL. Tom is sitting
in one of the booths shooting craps with a
native civilian. Roland rushes in, tells Tom about
the revolution, says:

SP: "WE'VE GOT TO SAVE ALL THOSE GINKS
I INSURED."
   He grabs Tom and they rush out of the cafe
toward the palace leaving the native flat.

116. CONWELL'S ROOM IN CONSULATE. Conwell, with his three guards, enter stealthily. He
places the three guards against the wall on each
side of the door leading to the Colonel's room
and he then knocks on the door.

117. COLONEL'S ROOM IN CONSULATE. Rosalie, terrified, says: "Who is it?"

118. CONWELL'S ROOM IN CONSULATE. Conwell says, "It's I—Jim Conwell."

119. COLONEL'S ROOM IN CONSULATE. Rosalie, greatly relieved, lowers gun and says, "come in." Conwell enters, leaving the door open. He smiles ingratiatingly and comes forward. She asks him if he knows where her father is. He doesn't know, but pats her reassuringly on the shoulder and gently takes the revolver from her. In this position he whistles. The girl looks up quickly and jumps to her feet in alarm, but before she can make any move, the three guards rush in and seize her. Conwell steps to her and says:

SP: "DON'T BE ALARMED, THESE GENTLEMEN WILL ESCORT YOU TO THE KING'S PALACE WHERE OUR WEDDING WILL TAKE PLACE TO-MORROW MORNING."

      Rosalie is horrified at this and starts to struggle, but the men hold her and start to take her out of the room. The old Mammy grabs a big book and lambasts Conwell over the head, stunning him for a moment. She then runs for the guards, jumping on their backs like a cat. By this time Conwell has regained his feet, grabs the colored servant and bangs her on the head with something heavy, then chucks her over into a corner and he follows the guards and Rosalie out through a back door.

120. BACK DOOR OF CONSULATE. Conwell rushes out followed by the three guards dragging Rosalie. They start toward palace but Conwell stops them and says:

SP: "WE'LL KEEP HER IN OUR RENDEZVOUS UNTIL ENRICO CAPTURES THE PALACE."

      They all exit in the opposite direction.

121. REVOLUTIONISTS' RENDEZVOUS. Enrico is there with the General, Major and Countess. Enrico is haranguing the soldiers, giving them final instructions. They all cheer. Enrico calls Major to him and tells him to look after the Countess and after they have captured the palace to bring her there. Major salutes and steps aside

with Countess. Enrico goes on haranguing the soldiers and at length says:

SP: "AND REMEMBER THERE IS A PRICE OF THIRTY PESETAS ON THE HEAD OF THE KING!"

They all cheer. Enrico draws his sword and says:

SP: "ON TO THE PALACE!"

He gives orders to fall in, which they do, then forward march. They all march out led by Enrico, the Countess and Major looking after them.

T: THIRTY PESETAS' WORTH OF ROYALTY.

122.   KING'S BEDCHAMBER. Councilors standing by bed all salute drunkenly. Two lackeys carry the King (who is dressed in a long white night gown and night cap and hugging a bottle of booze to his chest) and chuck him on the bed, cover him up and stand. The king dozes off into a drunken stupor. Councilors salute and stagger out toward Council Room (followed by lackeys).

123.   HALLWAY IN PALACE. Councilors stagger out of King's bedroom across hall and into Council Room.

124.   COUNCIL ROOM IN PALACE. Councilors stagger in and sit at table and begin boozing— drinking to:

SP: "GOOD REST TO HIS MAJESTY."

They all down a drink and sit down.

125.   FRONT DOOR OF PALACE. Two royal guards on duty (uniforms elaborate and different from those of the army). Roland and Tom rush up and demand admittance and are refused. Roland says it is very important to see the king, but they won't let him in. Tom wants to wallop them on the nose and go in, but is restrained by their guns and finally he and Roland leave in disgust and go down to the edge of the grounds, then look back and see the guards are not looking and beat it around to the side of the palace.

126.   STREET. Enrico, the General and soldiers march through toward palace.

127. WALL OF PALACE (outside). Roland and
      Tom run in and scale wall.
128. WALL OF PALACE (inside). Roland and Tom
      jump down and run toward back of palace.
129. BACK OF PALACE. Roland and Tom run in.
      Tom leans down and makes a stepping stone for
      Roland, who jumps from his back to window,
      pushes it open and crawls in. He then pulls Tom
      up after him.
130. HALLWAY OF PALACE LOOKING TO-
      WARD THE BACK. Roland and Tom crawl
      in the window, quickly look about, rush into the
      Council Room.
131. COUNCIL CHAMBER. Councilors all drunk.
      Tom and Roland rush in from hall, tell them
      there is a revolution on and they've got to beat
      it to save their hides as the soldiers and revo-
      lutionists are coming. They all get up in a
      drunken, stupid sort of way—don't take it in.
      Two lackeys rush out the window at back. Ro-
      land demands of one of the councilors:
SP: "WHERE IS THE KING?"
      The councilor, half soused, points across the
      hall. Roland and Tom stir up the councilors
      and drive them out into the hall. One of them is
      too far gone to walk. Roland pitches him over
      to Tom who throws him over his shoulder and
      carries him out. Little Frijole, the grouch, is the
      soberest of the lot and realizes the situation and
      tries to follow along, but Roland gives him a
      shove and lands him in a chair, saying:
SP: "GET AWAY! YOU'RE NOT INSURED."
      They all go out into the hall, Frijole getting up
      and following. As he does so, he draws an old
      revolver out of his pocket.
132. HALLWAY IN THE PALACE. They all cross
      the hallway to the king's bedroom—Tom carrying
      his councilor, Frijole following, waving his re-
      volver.
133. KING'S BEDROOM. They all rush in—Tom
      carrying the same councilor and Frijole waving
      his revolver. Roland rushes to the king's bed
      and wakes him up while the councilors stagger
      about stupidly, bumping into each other and not

yet fully realizing what's up. Tom drops his councilor on a couch or floor. Roland wakes the king up—pulls him out of bed—tells him that the revolutionists are coming and he has got to get out. The King is very stupid from drink and doesn't take it in. Roland shakes him and tries to make him understand.

134. STREET CORNER NEARER THE PALACE. Enrico, the General and army march through.

135. KING'S BEDROOM. Roland, trying to make old King Caramba understand, says to Tom:

SP: "GET SOME WATER."

Tom leaves. Roland goes on shaking the King. CLOSE UP OF LITTLE PRIVATE SIDEBOARD OR BAR in corner of room. Tom rushes in, looks for water but there is none. He turns and says:

SP: "EVERYTHING HERE *BUT* WATAH!"

Roland says to bring a bottle of something. Tom takes a bottle of champagne, knocks neck off of it and goes toward bed. CLOSE UP BY BED—Roland still trying to bring King to. Tom enters with champagne. Roland takes it and souses it in King's face—King falls back on bed. Roland and Tom pull him up again to his feet. King licks champagne from his face with tongue. They punch, pummel and slap him and finally bring him to. Roland tells him about the revolution—that they must get out of the palace and hide. The King looks around and sees the various councilors. Finally realizes what is up—asks where the Revolutionists are.

136. FRONT OF PALACE. Two royal guards sleeping on ground. Enrico, General and soldiers march in. Royal guards are overpowered and Enrico, General and soldiers begin to bang on door.

137. KING'S BEDROOM IN PALACE. Roland tells him they are rushing on the Palace. The old King is scared blue—begins to shake and tremble. Roland asks him if he doesn't know some way to get out. Finally the old King comes to his senses enough to remember a trap door under the flagging of the floor. He takes Roland over to the place in the floor and points down there.

Roland and Tom look and see nothing but flagging. The old King keeps pointing and poking with his toe, says:

SP: "STAIRWAY UNDER THERE."

Finally Roland taps the flagging with his heel. Then he and Tom get down on their knees and try to pull up the stone. It won't come. They look up at the King. He says, yes, that's the place.

SP: "TUNNEL — LEADS TO EL JUGGO PRISON."

Tom then gets a big jack-knife from his pocket, opens it and begins to pry up the flagging. The old King claps his hands and nods his head. Roland and Tom continue pulling up the flagging from the floor.

138.   FRONT OF THE PALACE. Enrico, the General and soldiers banging on the door.

139.   THE KING'S BEDROOM. Roland finishes pulling up the last stone. Tom chucks the stones under the bed. Roland then raises the trap door, starts to shove the Councilors down.

140.   FRONT OF THE PALACE. Soldiers still banging on the door trying to break it down.

141.   THE KING'S BEDCHAMBER. Roland is shooing the King and Councilors down the stairway. Frijole keeps butting in and Roland pushing him back.

CLOSE UP OF THE STAIRWAY. Frijole is trying to push himself down, but Roland holds him back and says:

SP: "I TOLD YOU TO KEEP OUT OF THIS— YOU'RE NOT INSURED."

But Frijole insists that he shall go and raises his revolver at Roland. Roland ducks and knocks the revolver out of his hand. Tom picks it up. Roland pushes Frijole over to Tom, who picks up the little man and drops him out of the window.

142.   FRONT OF PALACE. Soldiers still banging on the door—door breaks through and they enter.

143.   KING'S BEDCHAMBER IN PALACE. Tom runs to door to hall, opens it a crack and peeks out.

144. HALLWAY OF PALACE (front end). Soldiers
      rush in. Enrico is holding his soldiers at the
      door, through which they have broken, telling
      them just where to go.
145. KING'S BEDCHAMBER. Tom calls to Roland
      to look. Roland comes to the door and looks.
146. HALLWAY IN PALACE. Enrico giving in-
      structions to his men.
147. KING'S BEDROOM. Tom aims revolver at
      Enrico. Roland stops him and says:
SP: "FOR GOD'S SAKE DON'T KILL *HIM*.
      HE'S INSURED FOR TEN THOUSAND
      DOLLARS."
      He grabs Tom, closes the door and locks it,
      pulls Tom away.
148. HALLWAY. Enrico, with a flourish, leads his
      men down the hall toward the King's bedroom.
149. KING'S BEDROOM. Tom picks up his coun-
      cilor and starts down through trap with him.
      Roland quickly removing traces of the broken
      floor, takes a rug and pulls it to the back of the
      trap door.
150. HALLWAY OF PALACE. Enrico and part of
      his soldiers are beating down the door of the
      King's chamber—the rest going to the council
      chamber.
151. KING'S BEDCHAMBER. He closes the trap
      just as the door breaks open and Enrico rushes
      in with his soldiers. Enrico rushes to the bed,
      sees the King is gone, looks angrily all about
      the room, points toward the council chamber
      and they all rush out.
152. COUNCIL CHAMBER. Soldiers with General
      looking about coming in from door leading to
      other rooms where they have found nothing.
      Enrico enters, followed by soldiers, discovers
      there is nobody there. He meets the General
      and they are much puzzled as to who could have
      tipped off the King and let him escape. The
      General shrugs his shoulders, says if they have
      escaped, Enrico can proclaim himself dictator.
      Enrico goes to the head of the council table, the
      General on his right raising his sword and
      shouting:

SP: "THE KING AND COUNCIL HAVING FLED, SENOR DE CASTANET PROCLAIMS HIMSELF DICTATOR OF BUNKONIA!"
Soldiers wave their hats, officers their swords, and all acclaim him dictator. He starts to make a speech and says:

SP: "GENERAL, OUR FIRST MOVE MUST BE TO CAPTURE AND SHOOT OUR RENEGADE KING AND HIS COUNCIL."
The General approves and calls an officer and tells him to take a troop and go after the King. Officer leaves.

153. HALLWAY OF PALACE. Officer comes in, gets together his men, and beats it.

154. OLD STONE STAIRWAY WITH HEAVY WOODEN DOOR AT THE TOP. Roland, Tom, King and four Councilors stumble up the stairs.

155. HALLWAY OF EL JUGGO PRISON WITH HEAVY WOODEN DOORS AT BACK. Guard is sitting there half asleep. He arouses a little bit.

156. OLD STONE STAIRWAY WITH HEAVY WOODEN DOOR (same as 158). Roland still beating on the door.

157. HALLWAY OF JAIL. The guard, amazed at hearing the noise outside this door, gets up, unlocks the big lock and opens the door. Roland rushes in with the King on his arm, followed by the four Councilors, Tom carrying one. The guard is dumbfounded at seeing all these notables coming through the tunnel and asks what the trouble is. Roland tells him there is a revolution. He looks closely at the King, realizes who it is, drops on his knees and kisses the King's hand. Roland pulls him up to his feet and says:

SP: "I WANT YOU TO LOCK THIS WHOLE GANG UP UNTIL I CAN GET HELP!"
The guard looks at Roland then at the King and says:

SP: "LOCK UP MY KING—NEVER!"
He then kneels down and kisses the king's hand. Roland again pulls him to his feet, takes him aside and gives him a couple of pesetas.

The guard says, "Sure, that's all right," grabs the King and hustles him and others down corridor, Tom carrying his councilor. Roland tells Tom to stay with them. Tom follows them down the corridor and Roland beats it out of the front of the jail.

158. HALLWAY IN PALACE. Countess and Major enter, followed by Conwell, Rosalie and guards. They walk down the hall and into the Council Chamber.

159. COUNCIL CHAMBER. Enrico at the head of the table, the General on his right (Councilors' liquor still on table). Several other officers at the table and a number of soldiers standing about. Countess enters with Colonel, Conwell, Rosalie and guards. Countess is escorted by Colonel to Enrico, who kisses her hand and steps over to Rosalie, who is with Conwell. She is terribly frightened but Enrico leers at her and tells her she has nothing to fear. Then turns to the party and says:

SP: "LET US DRINK TO OUR LITTLE BRIDE."
      They all take glasses. Conwell raises glass to Rosalie and says:

SP: "TO-MORROW AT TEN."
      They all drink to Rosalie, who stands shivering pitifully. (Quick fade out.)

T: TOO LATE.

160. EXTERIOR CONSULATE. Roland runs in and rushes in the Consulate.

161. COLONEL'S ROOM IN CONSULATE—Old mammy lying unconscious where Conwell had thrown her. Roland rushes in, is alarmed at seeing the girl gone. He goes to mammy, raises her up, shakes her, rubs her hands and slaps them, trying to bring her to.

162. STREET. Tom runs through desperately.

163. COLONEL'S ROOM IN CONSULATE. Roland is giving mammy a drink of water. She opens her eyes and slowly comes to. He puts her in a chair and asks her what has happened. She pulls herself together and says that Conwell was there with soldiers—says:

SP: "THEY TOOK HER TO THE KING'S PAL-

ACE! THEY ARE GOING TO MAKE HER
MARRY CONWELL IN THE MORNING!"
Roland shows his alarm and anger, is stumped
for a moment. The old mammy begs him to save
her girl. Roland thinks for a minute what is best
to do.

164.   FRONT OF CONSULATE. Tom runs in and
rushes into the house.

165.   COLONEL'S ROOM IN CONSULATE. Roland is still talking to old mammy, who is describ-
ing what happened. Tom rushes in from Conwell's room, rushes to Roland and all out of
breath points hand and says:

SP: "THE REVOLUTIONISTS PAID THE JAIL
GUARD TEN PEZITS AND HE TURNED
OVER THE KING AND HIS WHOLE GANG
TO THEM!"
Roland is in despair at this news. Tom still
panting, says:

SP: "THEY ARE GOING TO SHOOT THEM
ALL IN THE MORNING!"
Roland is utterly flabbergasted at this, looks
bewildered at Tom and the old mammy and
finally says to Tom that they have Rosalie in
the palace and are going to make her marry
Conwell. Tom is open mouthed at this news.
At length Roland says:

SP: "THERE'S ONLY ONE CHANCE — WE
MUST GO TO PORTO PUNKO AND GET
THE MARINES!"
Tom and the old mammy are very much interested in this and urge him to try it and Roland
asks mammy if she is all right. She says she
is and tells them to go on. Tom and Roland
beat it out toward the front. She looks after
them.

166.   FRONT OF CONSULATE. Roland and Tom
come out and rush down the street toward the
station.

167.   DUNGEON UNDER PALACE. Squad of
soldiers bring in the King and four Councilors.
Tom's Councilor is being carried. They chuck
them in the cells and go out. Col. Bird looking
out of adjoining cell and demanding that he be

released. The soldiers spit at him and go out.

168. THE R. R. STATION—Roland and Tom run in and quickly enter the station.

169. INTERIOR R. R. STATION. Roland and Tom rush in. Roland asks the station master when the next train goes to Porto Punko. Station master laughs sardonically and replies:

SP: "NO TRAINS TO PORTO PUNKO TO-NIGHT! THE REVOLUTION LEADERS HAVE GIVEN ORDERS THAT NO ONE SHALL LEAVE TOWN!"

He laughs again at Tom and Roland. Roland looks at Tom in alarm then asks the station master if he is sure. Station master says of course he's sure. Roland steps out of back door. Tom starts an altercation with the station master, telling him he is too fresh, etc.

170. EXTERIOR BACK OF STATION. Roland comes out and looks around in desperation. Sees native riding by on an old bony horse, runs to him and tries to hire horse.

171. INTERIOR R. R. STATION. Tom and station master's argument is getting warmer. They are threatening each other violently.

172. EXTERIOR FRONT R. R. STATION. Two soldiers (officers with revolvers) ride up on hand car, get off and run into station.

173. INTERIOR R. R. STATION. Tom is pounding station master's head on counter as two officers enter. They see him, draw their revolvers and shout, "Throw up your hands." Tom stops thumping station master and throws up his hands. They make him turn toward front door and while one covers him the other talks excitedly to station master.

174. EXTERIOR BACK OF R. R. STATION. Roland trying to bribe native to give him horse, but native refuses and rides off. Roland turns and looks toward station and sees—

175. INTERIOR R. R. STATION. One of officers covering Tom whose hands are up, the other talking to station master.

176. EXTERIOR BACK OF R. R. STATION. Roland, alarmed, runs to station.

177.   INTERIOR R. R. STATION. Officer finishes
his talk with station master, covers Tom also and
they start to march him toward front door. Roland rushes in and fairly catapults himself on
the two officers, knocking them down. Then he
and Tom rush out front door jumping over
officers.

178.   EXTERIOR FRONT OF R. R. STATION.
Tom and Roland rush out of station and start
down road.

179.   INTERIOR R. R. STATION. Two officers
scramble to their feet and rush out front door,
followed by station master.

180.   EXTERIOR FRONT OF R. R. STATION.
Roland and Tom running down road. Two officers rush out, see them and both fire at them.
Roland falls and Tom stops to help him. The
two officers run up to them followed by station
master. They stick Tom up again and jerk Roland to his feet. Roland loses his hat and puts
his hand to his head. He has only a scalp wound.
Two common soldiers run in from opposite direction—attracted by shots. One of the officers says
to them:

SP: "TAKE THEM TO THE PALACE DUNGEON
AND LOCK THEM UP."
The two soldiers start off with Roland and
Tom. The officer says, "wait a minute"—they
stop. He speaks to the other officer who nods
his head. The first officer then says to Tom:

SP: "YOU COME WITH US."
He tells the two soldiers to take Roland off,
which they do. The two officers then march Tom
off to the hand car, followed by station master.
Arrived at the hand car one of them says to
Tom:

SP: "GET ON THERE AND PUMP THAT CAR."
Tom and two officers get on hand car. Officers
cover Tom with their revolvers. The station
master says:

SP: "WHERE ARE YOU GOING?"
One of the officers turns to him and says:

SP: "TO PORTO PUNKO."
At this Tom's face lights up and he begins to

pump like mad and the hand car goes down the track in opposite direction to one of train in scene. Station master waves his hand to them and exits to station. (Fade out.) NEXT MORNING. THE FATAL HOUR APPROACHES.

181.   PLAZA—FRONT OF PALACE. Soldiers are lined up in front of palace. Populace in native costumes are running about talking excitedly and reading placards which are posted all about.

INSERT—PLACARD (in fake language).

PROKLAMATIONIZ
BINGUS DE SPOLIO KAYITZ! ETC.

DISSOLVE INTO ENGLISH WHICH READS:

PROCLAMATION
EX REX CARAMBA AND HIS COUNCIL HAVE DESERTED THEIR PEOPLE. ENRICO DE CASTANET HAS BEEN PROCLAIMED DICTATOR BY UNANIMOUS VOTE OF THE ARMY. CARAMBA AND HIS COUNCIL WILL BE SHOT AT TEN. ALL TAXES WILL BE RAISED TWENTY PER CENT AT TEN-THIRTY.

The people are frightened at this and call others to read.

182.   COURTYARD BACK OF PALACE. Officer enters from palace with sixteen soldiers. He picks out ten for a firing squad. He goes to the wall and paces off a distance, then lines up his firing squad. He then takes the other six and goes back into the palace.

183.   COUNCIL ROOM. Enrico enters with Magistrate carrying a book. Enrico leads him across the room and says:

SP: "THE WEDDING TAKES PLACE HERE!"

The Magistrate says "all right" and gets ready.

184.   DUNGEONS UNDER PALACE. Conwell and guards with guns enter and open the door of cell and drag Roland out leaving old Colonel in. They lock the door. Roland reaches through the bars and grasps Bird's hand, saying "Goodby." They take out Roland, who has a handkerchief tied around his head. March out. Ro-

land then straightens up and marches out like a Sidney Carton.

185.   COUNCIL ROOM. Enrico and Magistrate are waiting (no guns on anybody in this scene). Countess enters with Rosalie who is terrified and completely cowed. Enrico goes to her, pinches her cheek and says:

SP: "WELL, HAVE YOU MADE UP YOUR MIND TO MARRY CONWELL?"
She weakly shakes her head and says she doesn't know what to do. Enrico smiles and says:

SP: "SO YOU'D RATHER SEE YOUR FATHER KILLED, WOULD YOU?"
She miserably shakes her head and says "No." Enrico pats her on the shoulder and says: "That's a sensible little girl."

186.   HALL OF PALACE. Roland, with two guards and Conwell, comes up the stairs and they march to the door of council room and stop. Conwell smiles at Roland and says:

SP: "I DID YOU A GOOD TURN, NOW YOU ARE GOING TO DO ME ONE."
Roland looks at him suspiciously and Conwell still smiling, says:

SP: "YOU'RE GOING TO BE BEST MAN AT MY WEDDING."
He then throws the door wide open and indicates the wedding party on the opposite side of the room, with a flourish. Roland looks in astounded and horrified.

187.   COUNCIL ROOM. Enrico, Magistrate, Countess and Rosalie standing opposite door. They all look at doorway and see Conwell and Roland. Rosalie stands transfixed with her eyes wide open.

188.   HALL IN PALACE. Roland stands transfixed, . looking at Rosalie. Conwell invites him in with a sinister smile and enters first, followed by Roland, who is followed by the two guards.

189.   COUNCIL ROOM. Conwell enters, followed by Roland and two guards. Conwell crosses to Rosalie but Roland stops near door, with guards back of him almost in doorway. Conwell takes

Rosalie's hand, tells her Roland is to be their best man and, looking tauntingly at Roland, he leans over and kisses her. This infuriates Roland so he cannot contain himself. He suddenly whirls, pushes the two guards in the face. They fall through the door out into the hall. Roland quickly closes the door.

190. HALL IN PALACE. The two guards fall through the doorway, sprawling on the floor.

191. COUNCIL ROOM. Roland closes the door and locks it, turns and rushes upon the astonished Conwell. Then follows a general mixup. Roland having to fight Conwell, Enrico and possibly the Magistrate—or the Magistrate might be an old guy who beats it out the window as soon as the fight begins. Rosalie tries to help by picking up a vase or some such object and hitting Conwell or Enrico, but the Countess stops her and Rosalie keeps the Countess busy by struggling with all her might. Conwell must be put out completely and Roland conquers Enrico and the Magistrate and would be a complete winner but for the Countess. While she is struggling with Rosalie and the fight is going on, the guards in the hall struggle to their feet and begin banging on the door. The Countess hears this and her object is to get the door open. She is prevented for some time by Rosalie but just as Roland has finished off Conwell and the Magistrate and has Enrico down and practically out, the Countess manages to get the door open and let in the two guards. They cover Roland and he rises and surrenders. Conwell and Enrico are pretty far gone but they manage to get up and Enrico says to the guards:

SP: "TAKE HIM TO THE COURTYARD AND SHOOT HIM!"

The guards rush Roland out—Rosalie collapses.

During this fight we see a long shot of Tom with an American flag and the marines coming down the street.

A man running to a group of the populace and saying: "The Americans are coming!" The whole of this group then run out toward the palace. This group runs to the crowd in front of the palace and yell: "The Americans are coming!" The crowd falls back to the other side of the Plaza and the soldiers guarding the palace look anxiously up and down.

Tom with his marines rushes into the plaza. The crowd falls back and the soldier guards beat it hot foot. Part of the marines rush into the palace, led by Tom. The man with the flag and the rest of them stop outside and guard the palace.

Also, during this fight the officer and his guard of six men take the King and Councilors out of their cells and lead them off toward the courtyard, line them up against the wall, tie their hands behind them, blindfold each one and are just about to give the order to shoot when Tom rushes into the courtyard with his marines, who chase the soldiers off and Tom picks up the King and carries him and shoos them all before him into the palace, having jerked off their blindfolds.

192.   HALLWAY OF PALACE. Just as the two guards bring Roland out of the Council Room into the hall and start toward the stairs, Tom runs in at front with his marines. The guards, seeing them, drop Roland and beat it out the back window. Roland greets Tom ecstatically, looks at his watch, sees that it is one-half minute to ten and says:

SP: "TRY AND SAVE THE KING AND COUNCIL!"

Tom wants to know where they are and Roland points down stairs and back. Roland tells twenty of the marines to come with him and the rest run down stairs with Tom. Roland leads his little bunch into the council room.

193.   COUNCIL ROOM. Countess is holding up Rosalie, Conwell leaning against the wall side of her. Magistrate is starting marriage service. Enrico is sitting on the table holding his head and watching the ceremony. The door bursts open and in rushes Roland with six marines. He rushes over and grasps Rosalie and tells the

marines to cover all the others, which they do.

194. COURTYARD OF PALACE. Officers just finishing blindfolding King and Councilors. They are all lined up to be shot. Firing squad is all ready—sixteen in all, now. Officer leaves King and Councilors and takes place at end of firing squad. He is just about to raise his sword when Tom runs in from the Palace, lets out a yell, and followed by his twenty marines rushes in. The soldiers seeing them, run like mad, chased by the marines. Tom quickly jerks off blindfolds and shoos the whole bunch—King and Councilors —into the palace.

195. COUNCIL ROOM. Colonel Bird and two marines run in. Rosalie rushes to her father's arms and Roland tells Bird to look after her and to go into the hall, which they do. He tells two of the marines to guard Conwell and the Countess and Magistrate. He then grabs Enrico, tells the other six marines to follow, and drags Enrico out into the hall, followed by six marines.

196. HALLWAY IN PALACE. Colonel Bird and Rosalie are waiting. Roland drags Enrico out, followed by six marines. They start toward the front. At this moment the King and Council come up the stairs headed by Tom. Roland grabs the King in his other hand, calls Tom and tells him to bring the King along; hands him over to Tom. Tells the marines to herd along the Council, and they all go toward front of hall.

197. FRONT OF THE PALACE. People waiting. American soldiers there. Roland and Tom drag the King and Enrico out on the porch, followed by Bird and Marines. The people become silent, not knowing what has happened.

CLOSE UP OF ROLAND STARTING SPEECH. He raises his hand while Tom holds the King. He points at the King, then turns and says:

SP: "MY FRIENDS, FOR TEN YEARS YOUR BEAUTIFUL COUNTRY HAS BEEN RULED BY THIS COMIC OPERA KING, WHO HAS NOT DRAWN A SOBER BREATH SINCE HE ASCENDED THE THRONE."

Tom holds up the King, to whom Roland

points—the King weakly protesting. Roland turns front and speaks again, pointing at Enrico:

SP: "LAST NIGHT THE KING WAS DE-THRONED BY THE MOST CORRUPT AND CONTEMPTIBLE GRAFTER THE COUNTRY HAS EVER KNOWN—ENRICO DE CASTANETI"

He points at Enrico, who grits his teeth and wants to pounce on Roland, but is restrained by guns of marines at his back. Roland looks triumphantly at Enrico, then front, and says:

SP: "THE FIRST ACT OF THIS TYRANT, ON ASSUMING POWER, WAS TO RAISE THE ALREADY EXORBITANT TAXES!"

The people nod their heads "yes" and shake their fists at Enrico. Roland points to Enrico and says, "Look at him." He then turns to the King and says "Look at him." Then he turns to the people and says:

SP: "IS EITHER OF THESE WRETCHES FIT TO RULE THIS BEAUTIFUL COUNTRY?"

The people shake their heads yelling "No, no," and to-helling both the King and Enrico.

CLOSE UP OF ROLAND listening to this demonstration, turning first to the King and then to Enrico, as if to say "Ah, you see," and then front again and says:

SP: "IN AMERICA WE CHOOSE OUR OWN RULERS AND DETERMINE OURSELVES WHAT OUR TAXES ARE TO BE."

LONG SHOT OF THE CROWD—Hearing this, turning to each other and expressing their approval of the idea, one or two yelling out exclamations of approval.

CLOSE UP OF ROLAND—Smiling, looking again at the men on his right and left and again speaking front:

SP: "WHY NOT CHANGE THIS GOVERNMENT INTO A *DEMOCRACY* LIKE AMERICA AND ALL THE *CIVILIZED* COUNTRIES OF THE WORLD?"

LONG SHOT OF THE CROWD, yelling approval, waving their hats and hands and (fade out).

T: AND SO A NEW REPUBLIC WAS BORN.

THEY TRIED TO MAKE ROLAND PRESI-
DENT, BUT THERE WAS ONLY ONE JOB
HE WANTED.

198.   FADE IN JUDGE'S COURT. Roland is sitting
on the bench all dolled up in a judge's rig. Beside him stands Tom in a policeman's uniform.
He indicates to Tom to bring in the prisoners.
Tom tells an officer to open the door.

CLOSE UP OF DOOR AT SIDE OF ROOM. Officer
opens door and the King and four Councilors
and Enrico file past the camera going to the
front of the Judge's bench.

LONG SHOT OF COURTROOM, showing prisoners,
Judge and Tom.

CLOSE UP OF ROLAND looking over the prisoners
and saying:

SP: "YOU ARE ALL SENTENCED TO ONE
YEAR IN PRISON—THIS COUNTRY MUST
BE MADE SAFE FOR DEMOCRACY AND
INSURANCE."

The prisoners all look at each other in dismay.
Tom steps down, starts to jerk Enrico roughly
toward the door. Roland raises his hand and
speaks:

SP: "TREAT THEM GENTLY, CHIEF. THEIR
POLICIES DON'T EXPIRE FOR ELEVEN
MONTHS!"

Then Tom takes them very gently and leads
them out of the room. As they go out, Roland
says:

SP: "WE'LL CALL THAT A DAY. COURT IS
ADJOURNED!"

He leaves by door at back.

199.   GARDEN. Rosalie waiting. Roland comes to
her. (Fade out.)